I Want to Die but
I Want to Eat Tteokbokki

I Want to Die but I Want to Eat Tteokbokki

Baek Sehee

Translated from the Korean by Anton Hur

BLOOMSBURY PUBLISHING

NEW YORK · LONDON · OXFORD · NEW DELHI · SYDNEY

BLOOMSBURY PUBLISHING
Bloomsbury Publishing Inc.
1385 Broadway, New York, NY 10018, USA

BLOOMSBURY, BLOOMSBURY PUBLISHING, and the Diana logo
are trademarks of Bloomsbury Publishing Plc

죽고 싶지만 떡볶이는 먹고 싶어 I want to die but I want to eat Tteokbokki
By Baek Sehee

All Rights Reserved.
Original Korean edition published by HEUN Publishing. English translation
rights arranged with Bloomsbury Publishing Plc through BC Agency.

First published in 2022 in Great Britain
First published in the United States 2022

Copyright © Baek Sehee, 2018
Translation © Anton Hur, 2022

ISBN: HB: 978-1-63557-938-3; eBook: 978-1-63557-939-0

Library of Congress Cataloging-in-Publication Data is available.

2 4 6 8 10 9 7 5 3 1

Typeset by Newgen KnowledgeWorks Pvt. Ltd., Chennai, India
Printed and bound in the U.S.A.

To find out more about our authors and books visit
www.bloomsbury.com and sign up for our newsletters.

Bloomsbury books may be purchased for business or promotional use.
For information on bulk purchases please contact Macmillan Corporate
and Premium Sales Department at specialmarkets@macmillan.com.

CONTENTS

TO THE READERS OF THE ENGLISH EDITION

Four years have passed since I published *I Want to Die but I Want to Eat Tteokbokki*. This very personal story, which I once wondered if anyone would ever bother reading, has been published in seven Asian languages and is now out in English. This is a fascinating turn of events, although a little intimidating. Because for all the positive feedback I had received, there were critical takes as well. My desire to speak freely of my mental suffering was matched by my desire to hide myself from it all. I doubt I could ever again be as candid in a book as I was in this one.

I hope you find points of connection between you and me on these pages. My desire to be of help and consolation is as powerful as ever.

Finally, I wish to leave you with some words that I find myself returning to whenever I feel myself growing weak. They are from an overseas reader of unknown gender, nationality, or appearance (I've never met them), and they are also words I wish to say to you, the people reading this book.

I love and cherish your story. And I am your friend.

Baek Sehee

PROLOGUE

'If you want to be happy, you mustn't fear the following truths but confront them head-on: one, that we are always unhappy, and that our sadness, suffering and fear have good reasons for existing. Two, that there is no real way to separate these feelings completely from ourselves.'

— *Une Parfaite Journée Parfaite* by Martin Page

This epigraph is one of my favourite bits of writing, one I often go back to. Even in my most unbearably depressed moments I could be laughing at a friend's joke but still feel an emptiness in my heart, and then feel an emptiness in my stomach, which would make me go out to eat some tteokbokki – what was wrong with me? I wasn't deathly depressed, but I wasn't happy either, floating instead in some feeling between the two. I suffered more because I had no idea that these contradictory feelings could and did coexist in many people.

Why are we so bad at being honest about our feelings? Is it because we're so exhausted from living that we don't have the time to share them? I had an urge to find others who felt the way I did. So I decided, instead of aimlessly wandering in search of these others, to be the person *they* could look for – to hold my hand up high and shout, *I'm right here*, hoping that someone would see me waving, recognise themselves in me and approach me, so we could find comfort in each other's existence.

This book is a record of the therapy I received for dysthymia, or persistent depressive disorder (a state of constant, light depression). It's also full of personal and sometimes pathetic details, but I've tried to make it more than just a venting of my dark emotions. I explore specific situations in my life, searching for the fundamental causes of my feelings so I can move in a healthier direction.

I wonder about others like me, who seem totally fine on the outside but are rotting on the inside, where the rot is this vague state of being not-fine and not-devastated at the same time. The world tends to focus too much on the very bright or the very dark; many of my own friends find my type of depression baffling. But what's an 'acceptable' form of depression? Is depression itself something that can *ever* be fully understood? In the end, my hope is for people to read this book and think, *I wasn't the only person who felt like this;* or, *I see now that people live with this.*

I've always thought that art is about moving hearts and minds. Art has given me faith: faith that today may not have been perfect but was still a pretty good day, or faith that even after a long day of being depressed, I can still burst into laughter over something very small. I've also realised that revealing my darkness is just as natural a thing to do as revealing my light. Through my very personal practice of this art, I hope I can find my way into the hearts of others, just as this book has found its way into your hands.

1

SLIGHTLY DEPRESSED

Classic signs such as hearing voices, intrusive thoughts and self-harming aren't the only signs of depression. Just as a light flu can make our whole body hurt, a light depression can make our minds ache all over.

Ever since I was a child I've been introverted and sensitive. The memories are vague now but according to my old diary entries I was clearly not a born optimist, and I would feel down from time to time. It was in high school when the depression really hit, which affected my studies, prevented me from going to college and compromised my future. Perhaps it was a given that I would end up depressed as an adult. But even when I changed all the parts of my life that I had wanted to change – my weight, education, partner, friends – I was still depressed. I didn't always feel that way, but I would go in and out of a funk that was as inevitable as bad weather. I might go to bed happy and wake up sad and sullen. I couldn't keep food down when I was stressed, and I would cry constantly when I was ill. I simply gave in to the fact that I was someone who was depressed from birth, and let my world grow darker and darker.

My paranoia towards others grew worse, and my anxiety spiked around strangers, but I became expert at acting like all was well. And for the longest time, I kept pushing myself to be better, believing that I could get through my depression on my own. But it just got to be too much to bear at one point, and I finally decided to get help. I was nervous and afraid, but I tried to empty myself of expectations as I stepped into the consultation room.

Psychiatrist: So, how can I help you?

Me: Well, I think I'm slightly depressed. Should I go into more detail?

Psychiatrist: I'd appreciate that.

Me: (I take out my phone and read off the notes app.) I compare myself to others too much then scold myself accordingly, and I have low self-esteem.

Psychiatrist: Have you thought about what the cause of this behaviour and the low self-esteem might be?

Me: I think the self-esteem part comes from my upbringing. My mother would always bemoan how poor we were. We lived in a one-bedroom apartment that was too small for five people, and there was another apartment complex in our neighbourhood with the same name as ours that had bigger units. One time, a friend's mother asked me which complex we lived in, the smaller one or the bigger, and that made me ashamed of where we lived and nervous about revealing it to other people.

Psychiatrist: Is there anything else you remember?

Me: Oh, loads. It's such a cliché to put into words, but my father beat my mother. They have this euphemism for it now, 'marital disputes', but it's just violence, isn't it? When I think back on my childhood, my memories are full of my father beating my mother and my sisters and me, smashing up the apartment and leaving the house in the middle of the night. We would cry ourselves to sleep, and in the morning leave the mess behind when we went to school.

Psychiatrist: How did that make you feel?

Me: Desperate? Sad? I felt like my family kept secrets I couldn't tell anyone, secrets that kept growing bigger. I thought I had to hide it all. My older sister made sure I never spoke about what happened at home to people outside our family, and I made sure my younger sister kept silent about the whole thing. Everything that happened at home was detrimental to my self-esteem, but now I wonder if my older sister didn't have something to do with that as well.

Psychiatrist: Do you mean your *relationship* with your older sister?

Me: I suppose so. My sister's love was conditional. If I didn't do well at school, gained weight or didn't apply myself to whatever I did, she would mock and humiliate me.

She's a bit older than I am, which meant her word was law. There was a money aspect as well because she bought us clothes and shoes and backpacks. She manipulated us with these bribes, saying she would take back everything she bought for us if we didn't listen to her.

Psychiatrist: Did that make you want to run away?

Me: Of course. It seemed like such an abusive relationship. She was full of contradictions. For example, *she* could go on sleepovers, but I wasn't allowed. There were clothes she wouldn't let us wear. Loads of things like that. But everything was so love-hate with her; I hated her, but I was scared she would get mad at me and abandon me.

Psychiatrist: Have you ever tried distancing yourself from that relationship?

Me: Well, after I became an adult and started working part-time, I made a decision to become financially independent from her, at least. I did it little by little.

Psychiatrist: What about mental independence?

Me: That was hard. My sister's only friends were her boyfriend and me, because we were the only ones who would cater to her every whim.

She once told me that she hated spending time with other people and that I was the one she felt most comfortable with. That annoyed me so much that for the first time, I said something to her. I said: 'I'm not comfortable at all with you. In fact, you make me very *uncomfortable*.'

Psychiatrist: What was her reaction?

Me: She was shocked. Apparently, she spent the next few nights in tears. To this day if we mention it she cries.

Psychiatrist: How did seeing her react that way make you feel?

Me: Touched, I guess, but relieved as well. I felt liberated. A little.

Psychiatrist: So your self-esteem didn't improve after breaking away from your older sister?

Me: Sometimes I'd feel more confident about myself, but I think the general mood or depression continued. Like the thing I had depended on my sister for transferred to my partners.

Psychiatrist: And how are your romantic relationships? Do your partners approach you first or are you more proactive?

Me: I'm not proactive at all. If I like someone I just know they'll think I'm fair game and treat me horribly, which is why I don't even like to show them I like them. I've never told anyone I like them, or flirted with anyone. My relationships are always passive. If someone likes me, I go along with it for a while, and if that works out, we make it official. That's my pattern.

Psychiatrist: Does it ever *not* 'become official'?

Me: It almost always becomes official. When I go out with someone, it tends to be for the long term, and I end up depending heavily on them. My partners do take good care of me. But even when they understand me and make room for me, I feel frustrated. I don't want to be so dependent. I want to be self-sufficient and be fine when I'm alone, but I keep thinking that would be impossible.

Psychiatrist: What about your friendships?

Me: I was very serious about friendships when I was little, like most children. But after being bullied in elementary school and middle school, I think by the time I reached high school I'd developed a fear of straying from the herd, and was nervous about friendships in general. That fear was reflected in my romantic relationships, and I decided not to expect too much from friends or friendships anymore.

Psychiatrist: I see. Do you find your work satisfying?

Me: Yes. I work in marketing for a publisher, running their social media accounts. I create content and monitor exposure, things like that. The work is fun and I'm a good fit for it.

Psychiatrist: So you get good results?

Me: I do. Which makes me want to work harder, and *that* sometimes makes me stress out about getting better results.

Psychiatrist: I see. Thank you for being so candid and going into so much detail. We'd have to do some more examinations, but you seem to have a tendency to be co-dependent. The extreme opposites of emotions tend to go hand in hand, which in this case means the more co-dependent you are, the more you don't want to be. For example, when you're co-dependent on your partner you resent them, but when you leave your partner, you feel anxious and bereft. Perhaps you're co-dependent on your work as well. When you get good results, your worth is realised and you relax, but that satisfaction doesn't last long – that's the problem. It's like you're running inside a hamster wheel. You try to get out of your depression through your efforts but fail, and this continuing cycle of trying and failing feeds back into the original depression.

Me: I see. (I am actually consoled by these words and feel like something is being seen clearly for the first time.)

Psychiatrist: You need to break out of this cycle of failure and depression. Challenge yourself to do something you had never thought possible for you.

Me: I don't even know where to start.

Psychiatrist: It's only the beginning. You can start with something small.

Me: Well, I also post fake things about my life on social media. It's not that I pretend to be happy, but I post things from books or landscapes or writing, showing off how great my taste is. I'm trying to say, *Look at what a deep, cool person I am.* And I judge other people. But who am I to judge them? I'm so odd, even to myself.

Psychiatrist: It almost sounds like you want to become a perfect robot. Someone with absolute standards.

Me: Exactly. When that's not even possible.

Psychiatrist: This week, I'm going to give you a survey – five hundred questions on personality, symptoms and behaviour – and we'll use it to work out what kind of new challenge we can give you to break your cycle.

Me: All right.

(One week later)

Psychiatrist: How have you been?

Me: I was depressed until right before Memorial Day, but I've been feeling better since. There was something I didn't tell you the last time, when you said it sounded like I wanted to become a robot. I have this obsessive worry about not inconveniencing others, ever since I began having high personal standards. For example, when I see someone speaking loudly on the bus because they're on the phone or something, it makes me really angry. Enough to want to strangle them. Not that I would ever actually do it.

Psychiatrist: You must feel guilty about that.

Me: I do. I feel so guilty about feeling that way, and about staying silent. Sometimes at work the sound of someone else's typing drives me crazy, and once I flipped and told a noisy colleague to keep it down. I did feel better after that.

Psychiatrist: But what kind of person would feel so terrible about not having asked someone being loud to be quiet? A person who is deliberately looking for ways to torture oneself, maybe. Most people are timid but the self-imposed pressure not to be timid makes you criticise yourself, even though you did speak out one out of ten times.

Me: I want to speak out *ten* out of ten times.

Psychiatrist: Would that really make you happy? Because even if you did manage to speak out ten out of ten times, I don't think you'd suddenly think, *Look at me, I'm cured!* For one thing, the reaction you get isn't going to be the same from every person. And even when you can accept that a stranger is in the wrong and you should move on, you're still deliberately making yourself responsible for correcting their behaviour. Sometimes the best thing to do with people who would never listen to you in the first place is to avoid them altogether. To right every wrong you come across in the world would be an impossible endeavour for any one person. You're just one person, and you're putting too much of the weight of the world on yourself.

Me: Why am I like this?

Psychiatrist: Because you're a good person?

Me: (I do not agree with this assessment.) I once forced myself to litter and talk loudly on the phone while walking down a street, but it didn't make me feel *good*. I did feel a bit more liberated, though.

Psychiatrist: If it doesn't make you feel good, don't go out of your way to do it.

Me: I know people have their complicated reasons for doing what they do and being how they are, but I find it so hard to tolerate.

Psychiatrist: If we have a habit of judging people from a simplistic perspective, that perspective will eventually turn against ourselves. But it's also all right to be angry once in a while. For example, think of a person you admire and imagine what they would do in such a situation. Wouldn't they be angry as well? They'd find this situation intolerable, too, wouldn't they? If the answer is yes, then allow yourself to be angry. I think you tend to focus too much on your ideals and pressure yourself by thinking, *I have to be this kind of person!*

Even when those ideals are, in fact, taken from someone else and not from your own thoughts and experiences.

And like you said, people are complicated. They may seem perfect on the outside, but they could be doing terrible things in the dark. You can put them on a pedestal and end up being disappointed by them. Instead of being disappointed, try thinking this way: *They're living and breathing human beings too.* This will make you more generous towards yourself.

Me: I always think of myself as weak, and that everyone picks up on how weak I am. That no matter how intimidatingly I say something, they'll see right through me. I'm afraid that people will see me as pathetic.

Psychiatrist: It's because of your anxiety. The moment you say something, you automatically think, *How will this person view me? Won't they leave me?* And that makes you anxious. Talking about it with them could help, but you have to realise that everyone reacts differently. You need to accept that different people will have different responses to the same conversation.

Me: Okay.

After you told me in our last session to try something new, I tried an acid perm. I like it, and my colleagues complimented me on it, which made me feel good. And that other thing you asked, about my friends saying my best trait is my ability to empathise with others?

Psychiatrist: Are you good at empathising with others?

Me: Yes, very. Which is why I sometimes hide it. Because it can be a bit too much for people, sometimes.

Psychiatrist: I'd like you not to give too much credit to what people say about you. The moment you set out to be more empathic is the moment it becomes a chore. That would result in your empathy decreasing, if anything. It's good not to fake interest in things you're not interested in.

Looking at the results of your survey, you seem prone to cognitive distortion; you tend to regard yourself as being worse off than you are (sometimes known as 'faking bad', where a person 'faking good' is determined to feel they're better off than they are). Your results indicate you're more anxious and obsessive than depressed, and your anxieties are especially high concerning social relationships.

You also tend to be passive in your views of women. You seem to think, *My role in society is being a woman, that's why this is all I can be.* You're blaming your circumstances instead of your personality, in other words.

These are the most significant results: you're very anxious and find it hard to function socially, and you tend to think you're much worse off than you are. You experience your state of feeling in a highly subjective, extremely sensitive and often depressive way. You think of your condition as highly unusual.

Me: That sounds about right. But the idea that I'm actually *normal* is somehow even more weird to me. It makes me think I'm just being full of myself.

Psychiatrist: Have you looked up dysthymia, or persistent depressive disorder? What are your thoughts?

Me: I did look it up. I've never seen a set of symptoms that fits me so perfectly. And reading up on it more, I felt sad. How awful it must've been for people in the past who suffered from it but didn't realise.

Psychiatrist: Do you really have to worry about these hypothetical people?

Me: Is it wrong to?

Psychiatrist: There's no right or wrong here. It's just notable. Because there's really no end to worrying once you set your mind to it. If you shift your perspective from *their* past to *your* present, you can start perceiving your personal experiences in a more positive manner. From 'How sad they didn't realise this' to 'How lucky it is that *I* realise this.' In the past, you didn't know how to label your symptoms, but now you know. That's a reason for relief, not for more suffering.

Me: That's incredible . . . What's the reason for these dual emotions?

Psychiatrist: It's like with your guilt. You want to strangle someone, and then you automatically feel guilty about having had that thought. Your own anger turns you into a guilty person. There's a desire to punish yourself, shall we say. You have this superego that exerts control over you, a superego built not only from your own experiences but cobbled together from all sorts of things that you admire, creating an idealised version of yourself. But that idealised version of yourself is, in the end, only an ideal. It's not who you actually are. You keep failing to meet that ideal in the real world, and then you punish yourself. If you have a strict superego, the act of being punished eventually becomes gratifying. For example, if you're suspicious of the love you're receiving, and so act out until your partner lashes out and leaves you, you feel relief. You eventually become controlled more by imaginary outside forces than anything that is actually you.

Me: I see. What about how I like being alone, but also hate being alone?

Psychiatrist: Isn't that just normal?

Me: It is?

Psychiatrist: Of course. The intensity of the feeling is different for everyone, but everyone does feel that way to some extent. We need to live with others in a society, but we need our own space, too. It's natural for these contradictory feelings to coexist.

Me: Do you think I have low self-esteem?

Psychiatrist: Extremes tend to connect. For example, people who appear arrogant tend to have low self-esteem. They keep trying to get others to look up to them. But if someone has high self-esteem, they don't really care what other people think about them.

Me: (This is a way of saying I have low self-esteem.) When I think back on the things I've done, it all seems pitiful and pathetic.

Psychiatrist: That might be because you've often behaved not how you *wanted* to, but rather out of a sense of obligation, or according to standards you'd invented.

Me: I'm also obsessive about my looks. There was a time I would never leave the house without make-up. Or thought that no one would look at me if I gained weight.

Psychiatrist: It's not your looks themselves that generate your obsessiveness. It's because you have this idealised version of yourself in your head that you're so obsessed with your looks. You've made that idealised version very specific and unattainable. Which is why you might think things like, *I'm a failure if I weigh over eight stone!* The only thing to do here is to keep trying different things, little by little, trying to understand how much change is comfortable for you and what it is you really want. Once you understand what you like and how to reduce your anxiety, you'll feel satisfaction. You'll be able to accept or reject what others say about you.

Me: Is my binge eating also relevant here?

lie was so shameful that I couldn't bear to put it into words. And that one lie ruined all of my recent efforts to change my ways.

Psychiatrist: It is. Because when your life satisfaction falls, it's natural to retreat into primitive measures. And eating and sleeping happen to be our most instinctive base measures. But the satisfaction from eating doesn't last very long. Exercise or outside projects can help here. Setting some type of long-term goal, in other words.

Me: All right. I'm going to start exercising again.

THE HEDGEHOG'S DILEMMA

'Extremes tend to connect. For example, people who appear arrogant tend to have low self-esteem. They keep trying to get others to look up to them.'

The contradictory state of longing for intimacy but also wanting to keep others at arm's length is called the hedgehog's dilemma. I have always wanted to be alone, yet always hated being alone. They say it's because I have strong co-dependent tendencies. I feel stability when I depend on someone, but my resentment builds up. When I get out of the relationship I feel free, but anxiety and emptiness soon follow. In every relationship I've had, I cling to my partner but also treat them harshly. The more I received from others, the more I'd get tired of them, and I'd hate myself for feeling this way. But then I'd go right back to being the cute girlfriend the moment my partner told me they liked me. I know that within the safety of a relationship, I turn more and more into a coward.

Which is maybe why I find myself unable to quit my job. It's part and parcel of how I've lived my life so far. The important question is not whether this is the right or wrong way to live, but whether it's healthy for me to live like this. I know the answer, but it's so hard to act on it. I'm needlessly harsh towards myself, so I need comforting, someone who is on my side.

2

AM I A PATHOLOGICAL LIAR?

I lie from time to time. To the point that I can't keep track of my own lies. An example: when I was an intern, I was at lunch with my boss when the topic of overseas travel came up. My boss asked me what countries I'd been to. At that time, I'd never been overseas, and I was ashamed of it. I lied and said I'd been to Japan. For the rest of the lunch I was afraid that my boss would ask me questions about Japan.

I'm very good at immersing myself emotionally, and I'm very empathic; I also feel pressured to be empathic, which means whenever someone would share an experience with me, I'd find myself lying and saying I'd been through the same thing. I would lie to make others laugh or to get attention, while simultaneously chastising myself for lying.

They were only little lies, inconsequential enough not to be detected – but there were a lot of them. Because of the guilt, I swore to myself that I would stop lying, no matter how little of a lie it was, but one evening while drunk, I ended up lying to a friend. The

Psychiatrist: How have you been?

Me: Not well. Not well at all, in fact. It was really bad until Thursday and I started feeling better around Friday and Saturday. I guess I should tell you everything for the sake of my therapy, right?

Psychiatrist: Only if you're comfortable with it.

Me: Do you think I'll ever be able to lower my idealised standards?

Psychiatrist: If you grow enough self-esteem. When that happens, you may find you're no longer interested in aspiring to perfection or chasing some ideal.

Me: Will I ever grow enough self-esteem?

Psychiatrist: Probably.

Me: I feel like I have a craven desire for attention. I want people to think I'm special, and this leads me to lie. When I tell a story, I tend to exaggerate because I want the other person to laugh, and when I want to sympathise with someone's story, I'll say, 'I've gone through that, too,' and lie to them. And I'll suffer from guilt afterwards. Which is why I'm trying not to lie anymore, even about small things. But after last Friday's session,

I went out for a drink with a friend, and I lied about something.

Psychiatrist: Because you wanted to sympathise with your friend?

Me: No. I think I just wanted attention. It wasn't the kind of story you get sympathy for.

Psychiatrist: Do you think you would've lied if you weren't drunk?

Me: I never would've.

Psychiatrist: Then it's just a silly thing you said because you were drunk. You can forget it happened.

Me: (I'm surprised.) I can actually do that? I'm not pathological?

Psychiatrist: Of course not. We often lie when our cognitive abilities become impaired for whatever reason. Like when we're drunk, for instance. You know how our memory or judgement falters after a few drinks, right? We subconsciously start lying to fill in the blanks. How many times have you seen drunk people insist they're not drunk? We also find ourselves announcing things that have nothing to do with the context.

Me: So I'm all right?

Psychiatrist: You're all right. When we're drunk, we loosen our hold on our own minds. We call this 'disinhibition'. Alcohol and drugs bring about disinhibition, which is why so many compulsive behaviours surface when we're under the influence, and we end up doing things we would normally stop ourselves from doing. So don't get too hung up over it, at least not for more than a day. Just tell yourself, 'I won't drink so much next time,' and let it go.

Me: I do think I feel bad about these things for shorter periods now.

Psychiatrist: Learn to blame the alcohol a bit, not yourself. You said yourself that if it hadn't been for the alcohol you wouldn't have lied, that you did it because you were drunk.

Me: But isn't that pathological lying?

Psychiatrist: No, that's just being drunk.

Me: Doctor, I'm so jealous of people who don't say stupid things, even when they're drunk.

Psychiatrist: Does anyone like that really exist? I suppose there are people who fall asleep when they're drunk. In those cases, if their ventrolateral preoptic nucleus didn't happen to be the first part of their brains to get drunk and make them fall asleep, they too would say ridiculous things. And the ones who wouldn't are those who have a high alcohol tolerance.

Me: Oh . . . Last week, you told me that the reason I wanted to be a just person was because I was kind. But I think it's because I'm *not* a just person that I want to be a more just person.

Psychiatrist: You've already defined yourself as being an unjust person. If you have unrealistically high standards, you will forever be creating reasons to see yourself as inadequate, as someone who needs endless improvement. Getting drunk is an example of that. We drink precisely to get drunk, but now you're envious of people who drink and *don't* get drunk.

Me: It seems so obvious when you put it that way! Also, I wanted to quit my job this week. I was so stressed out. On Wednesday, I went out for drinks with some friends, and my work situation happens to be better than theirs, and I even like my boss, right? But my friends weren't doing well, which meant I couldn't complain or seem ungrateful. I ended up just listening to their stories. But I have problems at work, too! And there I was, just sitting there and listening to other people's problems.

Everyone else has a harder time than I do, my friends, my colleagues at work, everyone, I think. But I felt like it was so unfair that I didn't get to talk about myself.

Psychiatrist: And you managed to hold in that anger. How should we let it out?

Me: I thought of discussing my work problems with my boss, but I'd been struggling all day with a task she'd given me, and it took me until that afternoon to ask her for help – she solved it straight away. And I was so grateful to her that I couldn't bring myself to complain to her. Because I know she's going through a rough patch as well.

Psychiatrist: Why are you so aware of all the hardships others are going through?

Me: (Realisation hits.) You're right. Wouldn't it be more natural for me *not* to know?

Psychiatrist: So, complain. Let others know how hard things are for you.

Me: I wouldn't know what to say.

Psychiatrist: Observe how other people are saying it. They're saying they're having a hard time – that's how you know, so clearly, that they are. But I think you're the kind of person who would ask someone who wasn't having a hard time if they were having a hard time.

Me: (I burst into tears at this point.) You mean I was just *pretending* to be kind all this time?

Psychiatrist: You *are* kind. There's nothing you can do about that.

Me: But I don't think it's kindness, I think it's just . . . being pathetic.

Psychiatrist: You're attempting to silence your own complaints by thinking, *At least I'm better off than them.* And the world is full of so much suffering that it's the easiest thing to find people who are having a harder time than you are. But once you do, you then insist on taking the extra step of berating yourself: *How could I have been so blind to that person's hardships until now?*

It's nice that you think of other people's feelings and pay attention to them. But I want you to take stock of yourself a bit. Of your own feelings. You should share them with your friends, or if you're sharing them with colleagues, you can say something like, 'I know I'm better off than you are in certain respects, but I'm having a hard time, too.' If anything, it'll make both you and the listener more comfortable with each other.

Me: I've never had that kind of conversation with my work colleagues. And it's not like my emotions aren't visible on my face. I'm bad at hiding my feelings. On Thursday when I wanted to quit my job, anyone could see I was angry. Which makes people stay away from me.

Psychiatrist: They probably just thought you were having a bad day. You have to make an effort to know yourself. You can't *not* make that effort and keep thinking, *Why am I like this?*

Me: Do I not know myself very well?

Psychiatrist: I feel like you're not very interested in yourself.

Me: Even when I keep a diary of my feelings?

Psychiatrist: Is that not more of a record of yourself in the third person?

When you're having a hard time, it's natural to feel like you're having the hardest time in the world. And it's not selfish to feel that way. Just because certain conditions in your life are relatively better, it doesn't mean you're better off in general. Take jobs or schools. It's great when you get into a good company or university, but once you settle in, the complaints begin.

Do you think it would be possible to think, *This place is perfect!* from the beginning of any experience to the end? Other people might envy you, but that doesn't mean you yourself will automatically be satisfied with your lot. Which is why you shouldn't torture yourself with questions like, *Why can't I be happy with what I have?*

Me: All right. On Wednesday I was happy to be relaxing with my friends, but it was only a half-happiness. Because someone has to say, 'It was so much fun yesterday!' for me to think it really was a fun time, otherwise I wouldn't think so. I'm constantly wondering, 'Am I boring them?' or 'I'm enjoying myself right now, but how are they feeling?'

Psychiatrist: I don't think being considerate of others is a bad thing. It's only a problem when you do it too much and start being obsessed with it, and I think in your case, it borders on obsession.

Me: It does. And it used to take a long time for me to fall asleep, but the pills you prescribed make me feel sleepy at the right time.

Psychiatrist: Do you still wake up in the middle of the night?

Me: Once around four, a second time around five in the morning.

Psychiatrist: You should keep your phone far away when you sleep. It doesn't matter for work whether you look at messages at night or the next morning, right? Try to distance whatever you can distance. Set priorities on your own.

Me: On Friday morning before I took my medication, I was anxious and couldn't get down to work on anything. The pills really made me feel better. I felt a little anxious this morning as well, but after I took the pills around eight, I felt better.

Psychiatrist: That anxiety could be a side effect from the half-pill you're taking at night. As long as you take your morning pills, you're fine.

Me: Won't I become addicted to them?

Psychiatrist: It's not the pills that make people addicted to them. Addicts come here for treatment as well.

Me: When I take my pills in the morning, I feel much better.

Psychiatrist: Enjoy that. Sometimes, despite feeling better, you might think the pills are harming your body, which could develop into its own kind of stress. Try to enjoy the present. Right now, you seem grateful and yet worried about the future at the same time.

Me: (Silent, thinking, *If it were that easy I wouldn't be here in the first place.*)

Psychiatrist: You are fine now, just the way you are. You might say silly things when drunk, there may be side effects from the pills, but you're fine. If the latter happens, all you have to do is call me up and swear at me.

Me: (The assurance that I'm fine makes me want to cry with relief, how embarrassing.)

Psychiatrist: So. What are you up to this weekend?

Me: I'm going to my movie club.

Psychiatrist: That sounds fun.

Me: It is, and it makes me a little nervous. I'm not into book clubs, for example, because I have a creative writing degree and work at a publishing house, which makes people have all sorts of expectations about me. I was afraid people in the movie club would think the same.

Psychiatrist: Why did you decide to join a movie club?

Me: I don't like to go out so I don't get to see many people, and aside from my close friends I only spend time with my partner, and I was afraid my twenties would be over just like that without me having had varied experiences.

Psychiatrist: So you wanted to get yourself out there for the sake of experiencing new things?

Me: Yes.

Psychiatrist: That's good. And do you try to meet the others' expectations of you there? That you're a very literary person just because you work at a publishing house?

Me: I don't.

Psychiatrist: And you're still not rejected by them. I'm sure some people might be impressed or disappointed by you, but I want you to concentrate on your reasons for joining the movie club in the first place.

Me: The movie they picked this time isn't really my thing. I have nothing to say about it. Is it all right if I don't say anything?

Psychiatrist: Of course. Just say, 'I didn't like it, it's not my thing.'

Me: But I'll be embarrassed.

Psychiatrist: It's just your opinion. It's not like there's any right or wrong to it. Of course, others may have their own expectations, or you may feel pressured to sound impressive in your critiques because of your studies and your job. But the moment you think to yourself, *Well, this is the way I am, and what can you do about it,* you'll feel much freer.

Me: Oh. Just the thought of it makes me feel lighter.

Psychiatrist: Wouldn't it be more fun to think of things like, *I wonder what we'll do after the movie? What should we eat for dinner? Who will I chat to?*

Me: You're right.

TODAY, AS EVER, I'M IN THE PROCESS OF GETTING BETTER

'When you're having a hard time, it's natural to feel like you're having the hardest time in the world. And it's not selfish to feel that way.'

It's definitely reassuring to be advised by a professional. Just like it's more reassuring when a nurse or a doctor treats your wound and tells you you're going to be fine, as opposed to when a non-professional tells you that. Even if I did feel like my psychiatrist was looking at me like I was fake-nice or frustratingly dense.

At the movie club, I did what my psychiatrist suggested and said the movie hadn't been interesting to me and wasn't my thing. Listening to the playback of my session tapes, I did marvel at all the stuff I managed to tell my doctor. I'd only done three sessions so far, and I didn't feel like too much had changed, but I decided to think of myself as being in the middle of a process. At home I was still stewing on my own, comparing myself to others and criticising myself for being so pitiful, but I didn't do it with as much gusto as I used to.

I was once told that you had to be able to write even when everything was all right, and I wonder if that takes practice as well. I only write when the weather, my body or my mind is dark. I want to write

refused to hold my hand, going through the motions while avoiding any contact. That's when I really started to feel shameful about myself. I was disgusting, ugly, like an old lady, a freak who should be hidden away from sight.

In middle school, my friends I and were members of an online community, and the anonymous discussion board was once plastered with insults against me. I can't quite bear to recall each and every one of them, but there were comments like, 'Her face doesn't look it but her body is quite fat,' 'You should wash more often, your elbows are blackened and disgusting,' that kind of thing. It cut me to the bone that I was being judged for my appearance like that.

That period disappeared from my conscious mind, but given that I have a habit of scrubbing my elbows every night and checking in the mirror countless times during the day to see if I have anything on my face, the memories must linger subconsciously. I am always worried about how I look to others. This self-consciousness has brought me to the point of recording my voice to hear what I sound like. Nothing frightens me more than the thought of someone mocking me while I suffer in pain.

Psychiatrist: How was your movie club?

Me: It went well.

Psychiatrist: Did you have a lot to talk about?

Me: Not really. When I said I didn't like the movie, the discussion moderator asked me what it was that I didn't like about it and I just said I couldn't put it into words at that moment. Then I listened to what others were saying about why they didn't like it, and that helped me articulate it. When I listened to the recording of myself later, I realised I did end up speaking a lot during the meeting.

Psychiatrist: Why did you record yourself?

Me: In the office, I record all my important meetings, and I record our sessions as well so I can listen to them later. I'm usually so tense during interactions that I have trouble remembering what was said.

Psychiatrist: Do you really need to record yourself all the time?

Me: Well, the purpose of recording our sessions is to have my own record of what happened, and in the other cases, I kept failing to remember the things that were said in conversations because I was so nervous in the moment.

Psychiatrist: It's as if you're keeping yourself under CCTV surveillance – to evaluate your own behaviour after every interaction. *Did I do well that time? What did we talk about?* Forgetfulness can be liberating, you know. It must be exhausting doing what you do.

Me: It makes me feel reassured and ashamed at the same time. Reassured if it turns out I spoke well, ashamed if I didn't.

Psychiatrist: I think you should start allowing yourself to forget and let go of things that have already happened.

Me: All right. I suppose this also makes me look like a robot?

Psychiatrist: Like a robot?

Me: Yes.

Psychiatrist: I didn't really mean anything significant in our previous session when I made my comment about you being like a robot, but I think you're putting a lot of meaning into it.

Me: (The doctor is right, I had kept thinking about the comment afterwards.) You're right. I keep thinking about what people say about me over and over again. I wonder why I keep up this self-surveillance?

Psychiatrist: You put a lot of stock in what other people think. It's because your satisfaction with yourself is so low. But your life is your life, your body is your body – and *you* have responsibility over it. Right now, you don't process the input that comes to you through a mechanism of rationality or mediation, you go straight to the extreme. Self-surveillance isn't necessarily a bad thing, but there is so much you can do with the input, such as rationalising or finding a different way to think about things – but you only do one thing with it. There can be so many reasons for something, but you're so focused on the result of it that you don't see the reasons. You keep focusing on, *I'm sad, I want to cry, I'm angry,* which only amplifies these emotions.

Me: (Crying.) Was I born this way? So prone to self-consciousness, to emotional extremes?

Psychiatrist: Personality has a lot to do with nature, but nurture plays an equally large role.

Me: When I talk to my sisters, we're all the same – which is why we can't talk about our partners together. We're all so extreme that we never come to rational conclusions. It makes me wonder, were we like this from birth? Or did something happen to us?

Psychiatrist: Perhaps your perception of reality is so polarised and extreme that you're only able to see your sisters within the framework of 'Everything about us is the same' or 'Everything about us is different.'

Me: You mean it's a matter of my perspective and has nothing to do with reality itself?

Psychiatrist: Exactly.

Me: Am I really that extreme?

Psychiatrist: It's not that you're 'that extreme'. You simply have a certain tendency. First of all, I think you need to spatially separate your work and your rest. If you were stressed at work, you ought to be relaxing when you're home, but you're sitting at home listening to recordings of yourself. This mixes up the two spaces, which makes you feel near-constant shame and anxiety.

Me: I see. You know, nothing really happened this week but I couldn't fall asleep properly at night. I'd wake up at four in the morning and I wouldn't be able to get back to sleep, so I'd put on a movie. It was frustrating how little sleep I was getting.

Psychiatrist: You must've been very tired during the day.

Me: I felt better than I expected. For example, when people call my name, I tend to blush. But I didn't blush at all this week.

Psychiatrist: How many hours did you sleep?

Me: About four or five hours a night, usually a five-hour stretch and then in blocks of ten or twenty minutes. It takes about forty minutes from my office to my apartment. It's a country road full of rice paddies, and my mind feels so much clearer when I'm walking it. Being at home alone makes me feel depressed again. I thought about why, and I realised it was because I would look at Instagram posts of people I'm envious of. I think that makes me more depressed.

Psychiatrist: What are they like, the people you envy?

Me: One of them is the head editor at a company I wanted to join. I once tried to transfer there but messed up the interview. She's beautiful and dresses well, and her employees look nice, too. I'm so envious of her, it makes me wonder what's wrong with me that I can't be like that.

Psychiatrist: How satisfied are you with the work you're doing now?

Me: I'm very satisfied, but I'm also a little bored with it.

Psychiatrist: Feelings of envy are very common, it only means you have ideals. But envy coupled with constant comparisons with oneself is something distinct. I think you're only idealising her a little, it doesn't seem that serious.

Me: What would qualify as serious?

Psychiatrist: It has to manifest in your behaviour. But as long as you can think to yourself, *I'm all right,* you're fine. There's no need to be too negative about envying others. It could be motivation for you to better yourself.

Me: You're right. I really respect my boss at work. When that respect is healthy, I think, *She's so wonderful, I'm going to follow her example,* but some days I'll think, *Why didn't I think of that?* And that depresses me.

Psychiatrist: We all go through periods like that. We despair and often gain new tools when we overcome that despair. And when you're depressed, your perspective changes and the same situation is interpreted differently.

Me: So my mood is important?

Psychiatrist: Your mood is extremely important. It determines how you interpret the random events of life.

Me: I'm not sure if I can change my mood for the better.

Psychiatrist: Not for the better necessarily but perhaps not to be so extreme? I think that's what you should focus on.

Me: But I can't. I don't think it's possible for me.

Psychiatrist: See? You're already saying you can't. When I'm sure you can. Look at how well you did this week. The week before, you said you didn't do so well.

Me: You're right. And there was one more incident. There was an article about the movie club put up in our Facebook group. It had a lot of likes so I clicked the link, and I was surprised that everyone seemed to have gone to good schools. The president of the club went to a top university, and he must've hired a lot of his uni friends when he started his company, because everyone there had gone to good schools. Learning this intimidated me and made me want to quit movie club. I try to avoid the topic of universities, I keep feeling both superior and inferior at the same time. For example, I might be in conversation with someone and getting on well. But if I happen to learn that that person went to Seoul National University, I immediately think, *Did everything I said just now sound stupid to him?*

Psychiatrist: But you went to uni. What if you were in conversation with someone who, for whatever reason, did not go to uni, and that person said something like, 'But *you* went to university!' What would you think then?

Me: I'd think, *What has that got to do with anything?*

Psychiatrist: Exactly. You go to university on the merit of your high school grades but depending on what you become interested in after that, the depth and breadth of your thoughts vary tremendously. Your high school grades do not determine the rest of your life.

Me: Absolutely.

Psychiatrist: When you feel like someone seems superior to you, you should try applying those standards to someone with different circumstances. For example, let's say you're watching television and there's someone being interviewed who hadn't been able to

46

finish high school because of poverty, but managed instead to get their diploma through hard work later in life. By the standards you're applying to the other, 'superior' person, the interviewee's qualifications should be devalued. But do you really feel that they should be?

Me: No. Of course not.

Psychiatrist: There you go. You tend to apply those standards when you're at a disadvantage, not when you're at an advantage. Now, obviously, societal class structures exist, and graduates of prestigious universities do have an edge. But at this point in your life, transferring to a different company isn't about your grades, it's about your work experience.

Me: I should really try to think that way.

Psychiatrist: You should try to stop yourself from reflexively falling back on thinking patterns you normally default to.

Me: I think I have to change a lot. I had a huge inferiority complex when it came to universities, which was why I transferred schools. At first, I was ecstatic. But your university name is just an external title. Despite getting everything I'd ever wanted, my depression continued.

Psychiatrist: It's a question of whether 'everything you ever wanted' was ever what you *really* wanted in the first place.

Me: I honestly don't know.

Psychiatrist: For example, you might have mistaken taking the train with your destination, losing sight of the actual destination. The whole time you were caught up in societal prejudices and norms.

Me: But I'm really happy to have studied creative writing.

Psychiatrist: That's exactly it. What matters isn't what people say but what you like and find joy in. I hope you focus less on how you look to other people and more on fulfilling your true desires.

Me: I've mentioned it just now, but I really don't know how to tell the difference – between what I really want and what others want for me.

Psychiatrist: You know how sometimes you have an inkling of something, even while you're saying you have no idea? That joy you felt when you studied creative writing and your satisfaction with your current work? I think those are your most honest feelings.

Me: Feelings that I feel immediately?

Psychiatrist: Yes, like pleasure.

Me: If I feel things other than pleasure, should I not do them?

Psychiatrist: Well, sometimes you need to do things you don't want to do, for different reasons.

Me: Movie club will end soon. Another club will be starting up, but I'm not sure if I want to join or not.

Psychiatrist: Why don't you write down the pros and cons of the club, you might find an answer there. It's just a hobby after all. You mustn't let your hobby become stressful. But I hope if you don't do it isn't out of fear.

Me: I have a serious victim complex. Even in this club, I kept thinking people hated me.

Psychiatrist: Can you give an example?

Me: We went to a bar after the club. I didn't want to get drunk, and I managed to stay sober at first, but then I ended up getting drunk. It was near the end, and I can't quite remember what happened, but I noticed the president and the moderator signalling to each other that someone should put me in a cab. I became so ashamed of this faint memory, and I got the feeling they hated me.

Psychiatrist: Maybe they were simply concerned for you?

Me: What?

Psychiatrist: Well, when one has a friend who's very drunk, one calls a cab for the friend so they can get home safely.

Me: Oh. You're right. Why didn't I think of that? They were concerned. As I would've been concerned for a drunk friend, too.

Psychiatrist: Usually before a dream becomes reality, we tend to think we'll wish for nothing else if only the dream is realised. Imagine how you'd feel if you always remembered that your dream has already been fulfilled. Everything that comes after would be like a lovely bonus. When you feel envious of something, try to imagine how you would look to your twenty-year-old self. Wouldn't she think something like, *Wow, look at me! I graduated college and I'm working at a publishing house!*

Me: (Suddenly burst into tears.) I would've been overjoyed!

Psychiatrist: To the point of thinking: *I want to go up to that person and ask her how she did it!* But the you of the present is looking at your life and past as if you're a failure. When in

truth, from the perspective of a younger you, you're the very picture of success.

Me: Sometimes I think, thirty-five-year-old me would feel so sad about twenty-eight-year-old me. And if I were to meet myself as a twenty-year-old, I would tell her something like, 'You don't have to worry so much' . . . But all that's easier said than done.

Psychiatrist: What I'm saying is, don't compare yourself to other people. Compare yourself to your past self.

Me: What about my victim complex?

Psychiatrist: We have to keep thinking through it. Because there are parts of it that have to do with your personality. You've lived with anxiety for a long time. Once your new experiences start overwriting your old ones, your view of yourself and others may become far brighter than it is now.

TWENTY-YEAR-OLD ME TO THE ME OF NOW

'What matters isn't what people say but what you like and find joy in. I hope you focus less on how you look to other people and more on fulfilling your true desires.'

I've always looked at the past from the future's perspective: how would twenty-eight-year-old me look to thirty-five-year-old me? Or twenty-year-old me to twenty-eight-year-old me? Now I want to go to my past me's and tell them: 'You don't have to try so hard.'

Back when I had nothing, no future or college or money, when I was doing menial jobs right up to my university transfer exams, like cleaning up after students in rented study carrels or working the counter at fitness clubs from six in the morning, when my face looked like a bleak black-and-white film still in the mirror – could that girl have imagined she would become me one day? That she would graduate college, work at her dream publishing house doing someone she loved? How happy that would've made her.

I've worked hard to get here. And now I make a living doing what I enjoy. I've no anxieties about whether this is the right path for me. All I want is to get better at it. That's enough for me – why did I torture myself by comparing myself to someone else? If twenty-year-old me met me today, she would cry with joy. And that's enough for me.

4

MY DESIRE TO BECOME SPECIAL ISN'T SPECIAL AT ALL

Psychiatrist: How have you been?

Me: Good.

Psychiatrist: Good, how?

Me: A lot has happened. I made a friend. We're very different but very similar at the same time. Different personalities but on the same wavelength, so to speak. Which is how we became close really quickly. I'm usually very anxious about relationships like this, and honestly, I don't have many friends. It's hard for me to get close to someone. I did have a friend during my last semester of university. She was in a different department, but we took the same fiction-writing workshop together, she was a good writer – which is why I first approached her – and we became fast friends and spent that entire semester practically inseparable. But I ended up

losing contact with her. You know how you think someone is very similar to you, and then as time goes by you see how different they are? She must not have realised what an anxious and petty person I was. She ended up finding me incomprehensible. It got to the point where I didn't know what to say in front of her, and I became cautious and lost all my self-confidence whenever we were together. After classes ended, I did a fiction workshop with her. That's when my resentment peaked, and I dropped out of the workshop. Which is how we lost contact. I didn't think that affected my emotions so much at the time, but since I met this new friend, I've started having flashbacks about that time. I keep thinking, *What happens if this friend also drops out of my life? She'll stop wanting to spend time with me if she realises what I'm like.* I'm so afraid of that.

Psychiatrist: But there isn't anything you can really do about it right now. Why not focus on the moment? This anxiety about losing something seems to happen whenever anything comes into your possession.

Me: Possession isn't the right word . . . I'm just afraid that when I start liking someone, they'll start thinking I'm a sucker.

Psychiatrist: Does she treat you badly? Is she the type to believe that if two people like each other, whoever likes the other person more is 'weaker'?

Me: My friend isn't that interested in anyone else, and I'm interested in people who aren't interested in others. Which is why it's so special to me that of all the people in our company, she would choose to be my friend. Special, but also pathetic of me.

Psychiatrist: Because you feel like you've been chosen?

Me: Right. Isn't that funny?

Psychiatrist: Let's redistribute your affections a little bit. Because you'll end up the weaker person otherwise. And the more you sacrifice, the more you'll begin to expect a payback. You'll feel that because you've done so much for them, you haven't received enough compensation for your affections, and that will make you even more obsessed with them.

Me: But I only *think* about it a lot. I never take action. I just sit around doing nothing, and then stew in my own disappointment.

Psychiatrist: The thought that you can't betray the person who has chosen you makes you feel obligated to them, ties you to them. Instead of keeping people at arm's length or living in the anxiety of trying desperately not to be discarded after a relationship is established, try thinking more in terms of, 'Am I really compatible with this person? What do I like about them, and what do I not?'

Me: She's really special, but I'm so ordinary and basic. That's the thought that really tortures me.

Psychiatrist: So you think she has specifically sought out an ordinary and basic person? A person who is so special that they have no friends in their company has chosen someone who is not special at all?

Me: Well, no . . . And I'm trying to be more consciously honest. I think a lot of issues would be resolved quicker if I were honest, and the more I like someone, the more honest I want to be with them.

Psychiatrist: Is there no fear when you show your honest self?

Me: There is. Which is why I like to start off by being as honest as possible.

Psychiatrist: That's a good thing.

Me: I'm glad you think so. I told my friend that, too. That I'm a very ordinary and boring person, and that I'm afraid she will be disappointed when she realises this. But she confessed she thinks of herself as ordinary as well. I was in a creative writing programme and work at a publishing house, so I see lots of artistic people. I don't really fit in with them. I'm just too ordinary, I think. But even when I'm meeting people who have nothing to do with the arts, it feels like I'm an island in the ocean. Someone who's neither this nor that. But my friend said she feels that way too. She said, 'I love art, but I also love trashy TV.' She said she felt like a minotaur, half-human half-beast, someone who is not an artist but not quite conventional, either. When I said I was afraid of losing touch with her, she said we both had our own lives and it would be impossible to always be in contact, but that it would be nice to think about each other from time to time.

Psychiatrist: Sounds perfect. Don't think about the future too much. Your anxiety can become a burden to others.

Me: Like my friend at uni?

Psychiatrist: It could become a similar situation. Liking someone and putting them on a pedestal can lead to self-castigation. Even if the physical distance between two people lessens, the psychological distance can increase. That can lead to feelings of inferiority. You think, *This person will try to distance herself from me,* and you provoke them into confirming whether this is true – either by asking the person, or indirectly. Your friend at university probably felt uncomfortable with that.

Me: People can tell I'm doing that?

Psychiatrist: It's a possibility. I understand this need of yours to confirm, but I think the way you go about it is perhaps a little . . . childish?

Me: Why do I do it?

Psychiatrist: For instant gratification. But that's just an instant. I think, instead of such methods, you might find more satisfaction in cherishing the fact that you've met someone you like. Once you start valuing the time you have together, does it really matter what kind of relationship it is?

Me: You're right. But how do I stop myself from feeling ordinary and pitiful?

Psychiatrist: Is that something we necessarily need to fix?

Me: But I want to love myself.

Psychiatrist: I don't think it's a problem that needs fixing. It's all a matter of how you see yourself. When you meet an artist, you see what the artist has that you lack. Why not change that perspective? When you meet them, you might think instead, *This person is an artist, how exhausting it must be for them to be so sensitive.* Or *I really can't connect with this person.* Different perspectives create different reactions. Right now, you're imposing your own standards on things and torturing yourself unnecessarily.

Me: I do feel I torture myself quite a lot.

Psychiatrist: Calling yourself ordinary might be a way of protecting yourself. It's your way of saying you're not inferior.

Me: That's true. I think those ideas have become stronger since I've met my friend. She really hates the idea of an ordinary life. And so do I, come to think of it.

Psychiatrist: But do you think what you consider ordinary is the same as what she does? There may be aspects of the ordinary you both think of as mindlessly old-fashioned, but there must be a difference between your two conceptions. You've got to stop falling into the binary trap of thinking you're either all-ordinary or all-special. 'Good' and 'bad' are not the only ways we think in black and white.

Me: I see. I like to be by myself a lot. But only under one condition: I must have someone who loves me. Someone must want to know how I am every day for me to be happy alone. When I was single for six months, I had a devastating moment when I woke up one morning and realised that no one was looking out for me or loving me. I still think about that moment from time to time.

Psychiatrist: If you make yourself anxious to gain attention, someone will give you attention. Then you get comfortable, and the other person will as well. But after that, you feel despair again. Despite your intentions, you start thinking, *If I'm happy then this person will stop paying attention to me,* which naturally leads to you trying to avoid becoming happy at all costs. This brief attention will alleviate some of your anxiety for now, but from a long-term perspective, it's just junk food that will spoil your health.

Me: My new friend also told me I should try being alone from time to time. To not rely on others so much. She said she had a period of being alone where she eventually came to the point of not caring if someone loved her or not, and she was totally fine. Will being alone really help me?

Psychiatrist: If that's your only option. But you don't need to seek that out. I think what you're proposing now is just another extreme measure. Your emptiness and fear are all mixed up, and you're asking for help to defend yourself. But if you depend on another person for help, it'll satisfy you only for a moment, and you may not be able to stand on your own two feet later. And you'll lose interest in new things or pleasures.

Me: Ah . . . In our last session, you asked me to think about what twenty-year-old me would think of current me. I really liked that. Something I thought about recently was how I used to love chaining myself to rules and regulations – when honestly, I don't like conforming to the standards of groups of friends. In the second grade, a girl named

Eunkyoung became classroom captain, and she was the boss of everyone. Leader of the pack. She got this other girl, Yoonjin, to walk her home every afternoon. I asked her, 'Why do you make Yoonjin walk you home every day?' and she brazenly answered, 'Yoonjin likes to.' So I turned to Yoonjin and asked, 'You do?' and Yoonjin quickly replied, 'Yes.' The next day, I was left out of everything. Eunkyoung treated me as if I were invisible when I talked to her, whispering to the girls around her instead. And none of the girls talked to me. For some time after that, I tried hard not to stand out or say anything out of turn, to just blend in. But I changed my mind in high school, and by the time I got to college, I went about on my own. It's the same at work now. I felt so proud of myself for that. I want to praise the younger me, tell her that she made the right decision. That I thought it through, made a decision, and did what I wanted to do.

Psychiatrist: It's good that you did what you wanted to do. I don't think the decision to be alone is something to be praised or not in and of itself. Because it's a matter of personal choice. But if you still have the memory of being happy having made that choice, that's good. That's comforting. You need to keep finding your own ways to comfort yourself.

Me: All right. I understand.

AN ISLAND

'I must have someone who loves me. Someone must ask after me every day for me to be alone.'

When you said you felt so comfortable with me, it made me feel pathetic that I was feeling uncomfortable myself. I also wanted to feel comfortable, to feel safe, to speak and laugh, but my words just crumbled in my mouth. Even when I was with you, I was a shadow. A dark, dark thing, stuck to your side, imitating your every move.

'This is so nice, this is so comfortable,' you kept saying, and I envied you for it. I wanted to laugh, to be comfortable in my relationship with someone, to be the kind of person who can easily become close to a person they like.

5

THAT GODDAMN SELF-ESTEEM

I'm oversensitive. That's the right word. I'm so sensitive that I overcompensate by being nasty about it to myself, like some animal goaded to the edge. And this contradictory emotion raging inside my body makes my whole sense of self crumble. It's become a habit to look in the mirror after I've had a bad confrontation along those lines, to take in my hot face where even my ears have turned red. My face looks pathetic and shabby to me during these times of inner war. Eyes that are bloodshot and unfocused, my fringe all messy, a dim and stupid expression as if I have no idea what my own brain is thinking. I look like someone of no consequence, an invisible person. My mood plunges, and the mental balance I'd carefully built up to that point completely collapses.

Psychiatrist: How have you been?

Me: I was fine and then not so fine around Thursday and Friday, and then I was fine again.

Psychiatrist: Why, what happened in those days?

Me: Remember that friend I told you about? You said me showing my anxiety to others could make them feel burdened with it. I understand that intellectually, but it's so difficult for me not to fall back into that pattern. You know how drinking sometimes leads to excessive honesty? I was having a beer with my friend on Thursday and telling her about that other friend I had in my last semester of university. And I ended up telling her about my anxiety, like I did in our last session. I regret that so much.

Psychiatrist: How did your friend react?

Me: Just, 'Oh, I see,' that kind of thing. Because I kept repeating myself. That made me feel extremely depressed and regretful late into the night, but I was immediately fine on Friday. You know how I said, when I like someone, I'm convinced that that person is going to think less of me? And I was dependent on my older sister, who also took care of me. And in most of my friendships I've been on the side of being helped and supported more than me helping or supporting the other. But this friendship is the first time I felt like I could do anything for the other person.

Psychiatrist: Do you see a lot of yourself in her?

Me: Not exactly. She's a little different. She's not used to showing her feelings. Whereas I think I'm good at expressing mine. How I feel, what I feel, I am good at articulating those things, but she's not like that. And she says so herself. I was worried she was someone who suppresses her emotions. I read something about that in a book, that emotions have something like passageways, and if you keep blocking your bad emotions, you end up blocking your good emotions as well. Your emotional tunnels become blocked. That really rang true for me. I told my friend that. But then my friend kept messaging me things that didn't seem important, which annoyed me.

Psychiatrist: You were annoyed?

Me: Yes.

Psychiatrist: You weren't annoyed with her last week.

Me: Right. I was mostly worried she would think less of me because I was treating her well. Which is why it was harder on Thursday.

The reason it got better on Friday was that I remembered how I tended to twist my own thoughts too much. So I said to myself, *Let's think about it differently!* And I concluded that this is just the way my friend is. She isn't exactly friendly in the conventional way, but she was sending these messages because she was comfortable with me and she liked me, not because she thought less of me. Another thought I had was: *So what if she thought less of me and was mocking me? That's not the end of the world.*

Psychiatrist: Do you think you felt bad because you'd talked about your friend from college?

Me: I really regretted telling that story on Thursday and chastised myself for making people get so tired of me. But my friend was so casual about it the next day that I was reassured. If she had been cold, I would've thought, *Oh, that's because I told her that story the other day.*

Psychiatrist: It's odd you have no middle ground there.

Me: I'm always thinking in extremes. Black and white.

Psychiatrist: You were afraid she would get tired of you, but it looks like you're getting tired of her?

Me: Yes. I'm not used to such contradictory emotions, which is why I'm telling you this now. And remember how you told me in our last session that my feeling of being 'selected' could create a feeling of obligation in me? I didn't want to admit that at the time, but I think you were right. *She selected me, she opened her heart to me, I have to do well by her.* I kept thinking that.

Psychiatrist: We don't live in some caste system, no one has the right to select anyone for anything. It's all give and take. Like in your relationship with your partner, you just go back and forth in being the giver then the receiver, right?

Me: Right, and because I hate that so much, I always end up with whoever likes me the most.

Psychiatrist: You're seeing a flaw in your friend, which is why you also feel a bit superior to her. If your friend's behaviour has been less than perfect, you can assume there was a good reason behind it and leave it at that, but you tend to go for the extreme scenarios instead, even when you know there are different ways of thinking about it. I think you tend to rank things and seek extremes in your reality. Which is why your behaviour changes when the other person's behaviour changes – to give as much as you've received – and that's going to be a burden in the long run.

Me: You're right. I ended up thinking, *I'm looking for a genuine relationship, but is my friend simply lonely and wanting to lean on me? Does she think of me as nothing but a crutch?* And as soon as that thought occurred to me, I said to myself, *I hate that!*

Psychiatrist: That anxiety could've made your friend more anxious. Because the other person can mirror you, subconsciously. It's like a magnet. When you want to get closer, they move away, and when you want to move away, they move closer. In general, thinking in extremes blocks out the nuances of relationships. You might have thought she was being annoying and enjoyed her attention as well.

Me: You're right. I was annoyed by her attention, but I enjoyed it, too. What kind of a pervert am I?

Psychiatrist: Why would you call yourself a pervert? Anyone and everyone can feel annoyed by and enjoy attention at the same time. Just think of it as your smallest way of guarding your self-esteem, that's all there is to it.

Me: So I'm fine?

Psychiatrist: You are.

Me: I've always lived in very small houses. You know how you can just glance at an apartment's balcony and guess how many bedrooms it has? I was so ashamed of people knowing this. But then I was ashamed of myself for being ashamed – which is why as an adult, I would just tell my partners or my friends outright, pretending to be all nonchalant. But I saw how my sisters kept lying about our house. I confronted them and said, 'Why are you lying about yourselves?' They replied, 'Well, what difference does it make if we do? It's not like *you* need to go around deliberately telling people how poor we are.' They said it like it was nothing to them when I had felt so guilty about lying.

Psychiatrist: But that's not unreasonable of them, is it? If it makes things easier for them.

Me: Oh.

Psychiatrist: You keep obsessively holding yourself to these idealised standards, forcing yourself to fit them. It's another way, among many, for you to keep punishing yourself.

Me: Do you think I'm getting better? In your professional opinion.

Psychiatrist: I think you're doing fine. Why do you ask?

Me: I feel like I'm getting better. I feel better at work.

Psychiatrist: And more than anything else, you have an annoying new friend!

Me: I'm annoyed all the time though. No matter who it is. And I'm so envious of people who think, *Who cares if this person doesn't like me, who cares if they think I'm annoying?*

Psychiatrist: Do you think every behaviour falls into a category of, 'They did this because they hate me' or 'They did this because they like me'? The whole point of not liking your friend's behaviour means you don't like her *behaviour*, not your friend as a person. But right now, you keep interpreting every behaviour exhibited by your friend as rejection.

Me: I'm always like that. Any reaction can make me think, *Oh, she must not like me anymore.*

Psychiatrist: Your mind immediately goes to the most extreme explanation instead of stopping to think of the many other reasons your friend could be doing what she's doing. You keep applying these extreme standards to others. In effect, it's your own thoughts that are torturing you.

Me: Yes. I kept thinking extreme thoughts, which makes me think I need to pursue a healthier relationship instead.

Psychiatrist: There is no absolute good when it comes to relationships. And it's perfectly healthy to have disagreements with friends and lovers from time to time. I just hope you learn to differentiate the parts from the whole. Just because you like one thing about a person, you don't need to like everything about them. And just because you *don't* like one thing about a person, it doesn't mean the person as a whole isn't worth your time. I think you should get in the habit of thinking differently.

TO NOT DEPEND ON DEPENDENCE

'Emotions have something like passageways, and if you keep blocking your bad emotions, you end up blocking your good emotions as well.'

I think I've come to rely on my psychiatrist. Until now, they were a kind of absolute good in my life: professional, and always ready with solutions.

I want to shed all tedious emotions. I don't want to pretend I'm special (although remembering that you're special is important in its way), but I do want to be happy. I don't want others' emotions or behaviours dominating my mood, or negative thought processes imprisoning me in the land of extremes. I want to break down all these repetitive behaviours that keep me within the constraints of rules and moulds. I want to own my own life. To do everything I want to do, so I don't live a life of regret.

Does pushing myself into extreme emotions make me happy? What do I get from objectifying myself and applying impossible standards to everything about myself? Sometimes I need to rationalise to protect myself. This desire to look at myself 'objectively' has been the reason I have put a knife to my heart for such a long time. What I need to practise from now on is to stop trapping myself in some formula of, 'This is what I have to be doing,' and to simply acknowledge the fact that I am an independent individual.

6

WHAT SHOULD I DO TO KNOW MYSELF BETTER?

Psychiatrist: How have you been?

Me: I've been well.

Psychiatrist: Did you feel drowsy during the day?

Me: I did, and I slept well at night. I did wake up two or three times, but I slept for ten hours. But while I'm fine when I'm drunk, I keep missing my ex-partner when I wake up. Why is that?

Psychiatrist: Have they called you?

Me: No.

Psychiatrist: It would be strange if you never thought of them at all. Because you *were* happy with them for a time. I don't think it's strange for you to miss them.

Me: And aren't people more truthful when they're drunk?

Psychiatrist: You don't have to read into it that much. We do get braver and more compulsive when we're drunk, and sometimes another personality emerges.

Me: (I hear the sudden sound of rain.) I think it's raining outside. My new friend is really influencing me. You know when you get close to someone, you want to share in their interests? I've been reading the books she likes and listening to her music, and it's been so good getting to know new books and music. And I'm going to take a fiction-writing class with an author I admire, beginning next week.

Psychiatrist: Are you going alone?

Me: Yes, and I also got accepted on the Brunch platform as a writer, which I'd been rejected from before. So that's a really nice thing that's happened, and I'm going to write book reviews there once a week with my friend [we ended up writing just one]. I haven't written any fiction in two years, but I put together an outline for a short story and that made me feel good. I made the outline thinking, *I'm going to be as honest with myself as possible.*

Psychiatrist: It really does help in many ways to use your imagination. It decreases compulsions in your daily life and there's an element of vicarious satisfaction to it. What about your plans to get a tattoo?

Me: I'm going to get one today.

Psychiatrist: Who are you going with?

Me: Someone I've never met before. I write a blog, just somewhere I set down my feelings from time to time, and there have been a couple of people who like my posts. So I connected with them and commented on their posts, too. It's not like I was trying to make friends or intended to share my life with them. But once I started writing about my therapy sessions, someone started posting encouraging comments. I once wrote something about feeling very depressed that day, and the commenter sent me a direct message saying they hoped I would hang in there and they'd buy me a nice meal sometime. I don't know why, but I found myself replying, 'I'll see you on Saturday, then.' I'm going to meet them this evening.

Psychiatrist: Are you scared?

Me: Not anymore. I guess it's because we've already communicated on a certain level, so I'm not that nervous. Normally I'd be afraid they were a human trafficker or something. But weirdly I don't feel scared this time.

Psychiatrist: Writing can be a profound way of communicating and understanding each other, but you do have to be careful. But as long it's your decision, it's all right.

Me: A little while ago I might have thought, *Meeting someone off the Internet? How awful!* Now it doesn't seem like a strange thing at all. But I should tell my friend to call the police if she doesn't hear from me after an hour.

Psychiatrist: Did you exchange numbers with the other person?

Me: We did.

Psychiatrist: You could pass the number on to your friend. Are you disappointed that your ex-partner isn't calling you?

Me: Not disappointed. I'm wondering if I should call them after some time has passed. If they really are serious about our break-up, I hope this isn't the way they want to leave it. Our last moment together was so pathetic.

Psychiatrist: Why do you need time?

Me: For the rage to die down, something like that. The sad thing is, I really wasn't looking down on them, but they think I was. I'm worried they're going to let that misunderstanding torture them for ages.

Psychiatrist: In any case, wanting to give closure is generally a good idea. But more than anything else, I hope you take this as an opportunity to get out of your previous thinking – that *This is the kind of person I should go out with* thinking – and see different kinds of people. For example, some people lose their first love and think, *I'll never find another person like them,* but after a while, a new person takes their place. Think of yourself as entering a sea change in life, and choose things you haven't chosen before – try to enter situations, even ones you know will end in failure, just to experience failure.

Me: I agree. Oh, and my friends like me much better now. They say I've brightened up.

Psychiatrist: Of course, how you feel about yourself is much more important than what your friends think of you.

Me: I'm just so wishy-washy . . . This week was a good week. I liked myself this week. I liked myself for writing again, for signing up to classes – and I had high satisfaction with myself.

Psychiatrist: I hope the tattoo goes well, too.

Me: It will. As you said before, there are so many good things in the world, but I always seek out the bad. For example, I was just dumped. I found myself thinking he didn't like me, but then I read something that reminded me that love comes in different shapes, and I shouldn't judge someone else's love by my own standards, which makes me think: *Right, they, too, must have many different thoughts of their own, there could be another explanation.* Then I feel like I'm rationalising and stop myself.

Psychiatrist: What's wrong with rationalising?

Me: It feels like I'm refusing to accept the truth.

Psychiatrist: It's a perfectly reasonable mechanism. It's you trying to find reasons behind your hurt or your decisions.

Me: It's all right if I use it to protect myself?

Psychiatrist: Of course. You're making a rational judgement. It becomes a problem if you overdo it, but there are many ways it can be looked at as a positive.

Me: A friend was once telling me about her dating life, and after I'd heard her out, I said, 'Hey, this is aquarium management!'* But my friend was completely unfazed by my reaction. She said, 'No, you just don't understand what our relationship is like.' I wanted to have that attitude, too. I've always depended on the judgement of others and relied on their standards.

Psychiatrist: Then you must first know yourself better.

Me: Right. But I really don't know myself.

Psychiatrist: Exactly.

Me: What should I do to know myself?

Psychiatrist: Many people think they're the foremost authority on themselves, but you should be more sceptical. You've got to ask yourself, 'Do I really know myself well?' Isn't it really like touching an elephant's leg in the dark and thinking it's a tree trunk?

Mc: What should I be aiming for?

Psychiatrist: To see all things three-dimensionally.

---

* Translator's note: In Korea, 'aquarium management' refers to the dating practice of stringing along several potential partners.

Me: You're right, so right. I think when you look at as many sides of a person as possible, you stop disliking them. I've thought about how I should be more like that.

Psychiatrist: The fairy tales we read as children are very one-dimensional. There are good people and bad people in those stories. But in the books adults read, it becomes harder to divide up characters into absolutely good and absolutely bad people. I hope you learn to look at a person as a whole before judging them. And to look upon yourself as a whole individual as well.

Me: Does writing notes help?

Psychiatrist: It does. I think this is an experiment you can act on immediately in your daily life, which is another good attitude to have. When you say you're going to get a tattoo today, write down your feelings before and after getting the tattoo. Once you do that, you'll find a commonality there. 'In some ways, I feel fear. In these other ways, I feel relief.' That kind of thing. In this way, writing can be a way of regarding yourself three-dimensionally.

'What's wrong with rationalising? It's a perfectly reasonable defence mechanism. It's you trying to find reasons behind your hurt or your decisions.'

Looking deep within myself is always difficult. Especially when I'm in the throes of negative emotion. How shall I describe it? It's like I know everything is fine, but I can't stop myself from endlessly checking to make sure it really *is* fine, and in the process I make myself miserable. Today was like that. I just felt like whining. And leaning on someone, and being sad. To me, sadness is the path of least resistance, the most familiar and close-at-hand emotion I have. A habit that has encrusted itself onto my everyday.

Things will get better with time. Or no, everything is dynamic, which means life will have jump-for-joy moments as well as bad ones, going back and forth like the tide. If I'm sad today I'll be happy tomorrow, and if I'm happy today I'll be sad tomorrow – that's fine. As long as I keep loving myself.

I am someone who is completely unique in this world, someone I need to take care of for the rest of my life, and therefore someone I need to help take each step forward, warmly and patiently, to allow

to rest on some days and to encourage on others –
I believe that the more I look into this strange being,
myself, the more routes I will find to happiness.

7

REGULATING, JUDGING, BEING DISAPPOINTED, LEAVING

Psychiatrist: How have you been?

Me: Not well. You know the friend I've been telling you about? I've gotten oversensitive about her feelings. I've allowed her to exert an extreme influence on my mood. I loaned her a book, and I was afraid she would mock my taste if she didn't like it.

Psychiatrist: Did she not like the book?

Me: She told me what she thought about it in a KakaoTalk message. It was a little pointed, I thought. I mean, even if it was pointed, she was criticising the book and not me, but I kept feeling like it was an attack on me as well as the book. Before I could stop myself, I sent her a message that said, 'You're arrogant and exhausting,' which led to an even nastier reply. I was hurt so I stopped reading her messages.

Psychiatrist: And how did you feel?

Me: I was more focused on the fact not that I'd lost a friend but that I'd met yet another person who looked down on me. It was depressing and I was so angry. I hated what a pushover I was and I hated her, too.

Psychiatrist: Your biggest problem remains this black-and-white thinking.

Me: Black and white?

Psychiatrist: Yes. You've backed yourself into a corner and made yourself choose between black or white. Whether to see a person or not, whether to be best friends with them or never speak to them again. You either lash out or endure. The only choices you have are yes and no, and there is no middle ground. I think with this friend, you thought you had a 'special friendship', which was why you tried to endure and continue. And you got exhausted at keeping up this ruse.

Me: You're right. At first I thought she and I had a lot in common but we're actually quite different, which was why we kept arguing. When she said something I didn't agree with, I felt like she was attacking me, and that hurt me. So that I wouldn't be hurt by her, I would either fit myself into her way of being or not make time for her. I could've opened up to her more, or maintained a slightly disappointing situation . . .

Psychiatrist: There are many shades of grey, but I think even there you think there is only one shade of grey. A spectrum contains many colours and shades, but you don't see it that way.

Me: I'm so embarrassed. I keep telling myself that people are three-dimensional, but I keep thinking of them as flat – which is why when I look at some people, I judge them as being such-and-such, and then cut them out of my life.

Psychiatrist: Think of it like this; you might like a writer's book, but when you're disappointed after meeting them in real life, you throw all their books away.

Me: Wow, that's true. When that encounter is just a tiny part of that person.

Psychiatrist: This problem doesn't stop with others. Your very real problem is that you bring this same judgmental attitude on yourself. Like when you berate yourself after a drunken night.

Me: I keep thinking that if I reveal a vulnerable part of myself, people will see that and hate it and leave me. But I know so many aspects of the lives of the people I love. Their bad parts, their good parts, their sensitive parts . . . Even if they have negative parts, I like that they have them because it makes them human. But when it comes to myself, I think the tiniest flaw will make people leave me.

Psychiatrist: It's your self-esteem. If you had high self-esteem and were sure of your tastes, you wouldn't care if people criticised you or mocked you.

Me: True. Can you believe how little confidence I have in my taste to worry about things like that? As if such judgement against me mattered at all. I definitely have low self-esteem, and that's why I'm oversensitive to what my friend thinks. And because I'm not grounded in confidence, I keep thinking every word spoken to me is an attack, and I see things as right or wrong despite the many other different ways of seeing them.

Psychiatrist: Did anything else happen?

Me: I realised something about myself. I equate affection with influence. Because my roots are so weak and shallow, I only feel safe when I exert influence on others. Which is why when someone is sensitive towards my feelings, I believe they really love me and our relationship is strong. But a strong relationship and an entangled one are different things, and while my head understands that a good relationship is two people with a clear sense of individuality working together as a team, my heart feels that if the other person seems very independent of me – as in, they don't seem to be deeply affected or touched by my every word, don't try to adhere strictly to my standards of behaviour, don't change according to my directives or follow my examples – there's something wrong with me. (I'm such a weirdo!)

Psychiatrist: It's this behaviour that feeds into your desire to be validated. The more you want to be influenced, the more you will try to influence others, and the less someone reacts to your efforts, the more you make an effort. And then you become exhausted. This is just another extreme effort, another way of creating limits for yourself. The idea that a person loves you only when they're influenced by you – that in itself is an extreme attitude.

Me: Then what can I do about it?

Psychiatrist: Focus on yourself more. Specifically, write down what you really enjoy, and also write about the differences in how you see yourself and how others see you. It would also be a good idea to take stock of things that you would do under the imagined gaze of others.

Me: But I always do what I want to do.

Psychiatrist: Do you really behave the same with everyone?

Me: No. I think I did change my behaviour for that friend a little bit. I don't know why I did that. I kept seeing myself behave in a way that just wasn't me, and when I tried not to act that way, I felt like I was being rude.

Psychiatrist: What if that rudeness is a way of expressing yourself? Take control and responsibility for your actions instead of caring so much about what other people think. Right now, your relationship is narrow, like a triangle, and pierces your heart, but at least a dodecahedron is closer to a circle than an octagon, right? The deeper and more varied relationships you have, the rounder your mind will be, and the less the angles will pierce you. You will be just fine.

Me: (Tears of joy.) Yes. Thank you.

*

THE TRUTH OF THAT DAY AND THE TRUTH OF LIFE

'To tell the truth, no one was looking down on me except myself.'

That human beings are three-dimensional is perhaps my favourite thing to say. But it is also likely the last thing I will remember in a bad moment. Everyone has multiple sides to them, happiness and unhappiness coexist, and everything is relative. To tell the truth, no one was looking down on me except myself. When I looked again at my friend's messages from that day, it struck me that her comment was just something I could've ignored. But because I had assumed she was looking down on me, the message had taken on a bigger meaning. Which is why I provoked her with a harsh reply. I wanted to get a strong reaction from her. I did it to end the relationship.

I hope that people who keep ending their relationships because they feel like they're being looked down on, people who tend to think in extremes like me, will read this. We are many-sided. That's all. We can't continue a relationship or end it because of just one thing. I understand this with my head, but my heart has more trouble recognising it. The unhappiness floats to the top like oil while the happiness sinks below. But the container that holds both is what we call life, and that's where I find solace and joy. I'm sad, but I'm alive, and living through it. That is my solace and my joy.

8

MEDICATION SIDE EFFECTS

I used to love being alone. Lying in my bed as I read or daydreamed, taking walks, listening to music on the bus or subway, napping, all of these were my favourite times of the day. But for the past two weeks, I've felt inundated by a strange feeling called 'boredom'.

I'd never suffered such tedium in the office before. Barely able to concentrate on anything, I found myself unable even to sit still for anything longer than a minute. In the end, I took the afternoon off on Friday. But even as I sat at home that afternoon, I felt anxious beyond belief and I couldn't stand the tedium. That's when I wondered if it was a side effect from my medication, and went to the clinic, where my suspicions were confirmed. The diagnosis made me feel almost bereft: my medication had given me akathisia.

Akathisia refers to the inability to sit still. You find yourself standing or fidgeting or pacing – it's an occasional side effect in people who take tranquillisers.

Me: Is it possible to develop tolerance to medication?

Psychiatrist: There are drugs we develop tolerance for, yes.

Me: When would I start to notice that? Normally when I take my pills, I feel calmer, more relaxed, but now I feel so tense. I keep feeling that tension as tedium. I haven't concentrated at work in a month, and if I don't find something to do, I feel I'm going to die of boredom. Even in the half-hour I spend commuting on the bus. Is this a side effect?

Psychiatrist: Indeed, it is. I think it's because we raised the dosage the last time. So you're finding it difficult to sit still?

Me: It's very difficult. So, so, so difficult.

Psychiatrist: You should've phoned me!

Me: I thought I must really hate work right now, which is why I'm so sensitive to boredom, but then I had a sudden realisation that this might be a side effect.

Psychiatrist: I think it's because the pill you used to take just half of has since been increased to a whole.

Me: I feel awful.

Psychiatrist: How is your sleep?

Me: If I don't take a sleeping pill or have a drink beforehand, the tension and boredom keep me from falling asleep. After which I wake up easily in the middle of the night, it's so frustrating that I feel like I'll go mad. Being drunk helps.

Psychiatrist: Alcohol can mitigate the side effects of that particular drug . . .

Me: It made me think I was dependent on alcohol and medications.

Psychiatrist: You must be having a very hard time.

Me: I have been. It feels different from depression. I think I'm just very slow at becoming aware of things. And ever since I started on the medication, I find myself unable to nap. Even when I do nap, my sleep is so shallow that I can't tell if it's reality or a dream.

Psychiatrist: Let me give you a pill now. How have you been emotionally?

Me: Oversensitive.

Psychiatrist: That was inevitable. Did you squeeze in any exercise?

Me: No, I didn't. I just walked home from work. That gave me some relief. Even when I was in the office, I kept going outside. Why didn't you tell me I might have side effects like these?

Psychiatrist: Well, you had been taking that pill already. We did raise the dosage a bit, which usually doesn't bring about side effects. You were also prescribed medications for the morning and evening, which were supposed to mitigate side effects. Did you feel any better after your morning pill?

Me: I did. But I was sleepy. It really was a very difficult situation. In my diary, all I could write were things like, 'I'm nervous and anxious and I can't stand it.'

Psychiatrist: What did you think was the reason?

Me: At first I thought I was turning into an active person. But even after craving time alone, I would only feel momentarily happy when I actually got it, and the boredom continued. I could feel I was on edge and my relationships with others were deteriorating.

Psychiatrist: You don't feel well, which is why you're on edge. When you came here two weeks ago, I increased your dosage to prevent you from falling into the old rut of your negative thoughts; I hadn't predicted your body would react this way.

Me: Is it something that can be calibrated?

Psychiatrist: Absolutely.

Me: If I don't take my medication, I immediately feel anxious, which makes me worry that I'll have to take pills for the rest of my life.

Psychiatrist: It's been three months since you've started taking these pills. Normally your treatment time depends on your symptoms, but the less time you've had your condition, the shorter the treatment period. I think you should prepare for a long game.

Me: All right. I feel like I talk about the same problem every time. And you always give me the same answers. I don't change myself, which is why the same problems keep coming up.

Psychiatrist: What you just said is very important. These are all behaviours you had no awareness of until recently, and to realise that you make the same choices time and time again is, in itself, proof you're getting better.

Me: It's all from having no middle ground and thinking in black and white. Which is why I wanted to make a middle-ground choice. I didn't want to end my relationship with my friend in such a destructive way, so I told her everything. That I had thought she was looking down on me, and that I'm so used to being extreme that I thought the only thing to do in the situation was to either understand her or end the friendship. Once I told her that, I felt much better inside, and my friend was understanding.

Psychiatrist: Good. This may be a kind of relationship that you have never had before. This kind of behaviour is how you increase your freedom and share your responsibilities with others. You should be very proud that you approached her and expressed yourself in words to her. And I think that incident with her and some of these recent feelings can safely be put down to side effects of the medication.

Me: I feel relieved. I couldn't work at all recently! It was truly a bad side effect.

Psychiatrist: In professional parlance, it's called akathisia, an inability to sit still.

Me: An inability to sit still! That's so funny. Through it all I kept thinking I shouldn't just be sitting still, I kept myself busy with all sorts of little chores. I'm a marketer, and I want to move into editorial so I started taking editing classes.

Psychiatrist: Was that a lot of work?

Me: It was. I think the only reason I could go through with it was because I drank a little before classes. But I definitely have fun planning books. I wrote three pages of a book proposal and really enjoyed it. I'm planning to write my own book, too. These are the things that made me feel a bit better.

Psychiatrist: I wonder if your desire for a tattoo is also a side effect of the drug?

Me: I'm not sure. I did plan it for a long time, but there was a bit of a feeling of *Let's get it over with* when I actually got there.

Psychiatrist: Did you get only one arm tattooed?

Me: Yes.

Psychiatrist: I'd like to ask: Recently, when you want your love to be confirmed, how do you ask for it?

Me: I say I feel anxious. I say, 'Do you like me?' or 'I don't know if you like me, I'm anxious.' Something like that.

Psychiatrist: At least you're expressing it. I do think the medication had a profound effect on the condition of your mind and body.

MEANINGFUL EVEN IN A SMALL WAY

'These were all behaviours you had no awareness of until recently, and to make the realisation that you always make the same choices is, in itself, proof you're getting better.'

I always considered pain or discomfort as me being a nuisance. I would censor my own pain. Despite my discomfort, I cared more about how I appeared to others. I hated to look as if I was whining about something that was actually more or less bearable. I was ashamed of my pain. Which was why it took so long for me to acknowledge the side effects of the medicine.

I always consider myself as unhappy, and know that's a form of self-pity, but today I want to console myself. I am always the target of my own criticism – not saying I hurt even when I do, admitting something is wrong only when my mind and body scream at me in different ways, and making the fact that I hurt in the first place my own fault. Even when I throw myself at others, I deliberately do it to get stabbed in the heart. Which means, the more I hurt others, the bigger my own wounds become. But I am trying to create a middle ground in my world, and I'm realising some of the ways side effects manifest in my behaviour, so I would call this past week a pretty meaningful one.

9

OBSESSION WITH APPEARANCES AND HISTRIONIC PERSONALITY DISORDER

Psychiatrist: How was your week?

Me: Better. (My side effects have eased off.)

Psychiatrist: What's been the reaction from people around you?

Me: The week before I'd kept talking to my colleagues about quitting. When I told my friend about the side effects, she said she'd thought it was because I was having problems at work or something. I asked my new partner, 'Have I been oversensitive lately?' and they said I wasn't at all, which made me feel good.

Psychiatrist: And it means you didn't feel good the week before.

Me: It was quite bad. But I still find myself bored at work.

Psychiatrist: Did anything in particular happen?

Me: Not really. I actually wanted to talk to you about something I've never discussed with anyone before. You might think it's nothing, but I have a huge inferiority complex about it. You know how I have low self-esteem. I think it's why I care so much about how I look to others. This is very embarrassing, but I am absolutely obsessed with the way I look. I hate my face. For example, I can't bear to meet my partner's friends because I'm afraid they'll think I'm ugly.

Psychiatrist: Is that how you are with other people's appearances as well?

Me: Do you mean do I judge other people's appearances?

Psychiatrist: Yes.

Me: Yes. I judge them. Because my own face gets judged a lot.

Psychiatrist: What do you mean exactly when you say you get judged? How does it feel to you?

Me: I know it sounds odd, but I feel like it's something being done to me. Like violence. I can ignore it, but the words really cut into me. Which is why I don't want to talk about looks with anyone. I know I sound a little all over the place right now, but it's because I find it so difficult to be candid about this, so I'm just going to say what I feel in one go. Women say I'm pretty a lot, but not men. I'm not popular with them. For example, women will introduce me by saying something like, 'Sehee is the prettiest girl in our company,' and I hate that so much. Because it puts all this scrutiny on my face. Last summer, I went to see a friend and her male friend, and she introduced me to him as the prettiest girl at our publishing house. So I said to her, 'Why would you say that! It's not even true!' And my friend said, 'Why shouldn't I say that? It's just an opinion,' and changed the subject. But the man really embarrassed me. 'They say you're the prettiest girl in your company?' Like he was mocking me.

Psychiatrist: Did it feel like he was mocking you?

Me: That's the way it felt to me. He added, 'But you're not really my type.' I was really angry at that. This kind of thing keeps happening to me. Which is why I keep thinking, maybe I just don't have the kind of face men like? Which is hard to accept, and which I hate, and which I kept feeling self-conscious about, which led to a whole inferiority complex. Do you know what I mean?

Psychiatrist: I do.

Me: Then why are you looking at me like that? (Note how snippy I'm getting.)

Psychiatrist: It just seems a little convoluted.

Me: My partner says I'm their ideal woman. Which means I'm beautiful to them. Which is why they keep talking about me to their friends, which makes me more and more hesitant to meet them. Yesterday, I took my dog for a walk and dropped by their house. They live with two of their friends from college. I thought there was no one else at the house but the two roommates were there. I hadn't put on any make-up, and my heart kept pounding and I couldn't look them in the eye. Which is why I just said hi and ran out of there as fast as I could. I messaged my partner, 'I felt shy all of a sudden, there were all those people,' and they messaged back, 'Sure, you must've been taken aback, I should've been more considerate,' but I just felt so mortified by the whole encounter.

Psychiatrist: Do you feel like you have to satisfy everyone's expectations of how you should look?

Me: That would be impossible, everyone has their own ideas of what beauty looks like. I know that in my brain, I just can't feel it. You have no idea how much I've criticised myself over this problem. Not even celebrities can please everyone. So what makes me so special that everyone should say I'm pretty? I know that makes no sense, and I hate it so much, but I can't seem to fix the problem.

Psychiatrist: What do you think of your own looks? You said just now that women say you're beautiful but you aren't popular with men. Are you saying you see yourself from men's perspective?

Me: Yes. It's the reason I hate my face.

Psychiatrist: To the extent of considering surgery?

Me: I wanted to fix my nose and shave my cheekbones.

Psychiatrist: Did you go as far as to get a consultation?

Me: I did. With a plastic surgeon and everything.

Psychiatrist: What made you not go ahead with it?

Me: I thought, *Is all this really necessary? Can't I just accept and love my face the way it is?*

Psychiatrist: Have you ever thought, *It's pretty enough the way it is?*

Me: Sometimes I do, but mostly not. And I'm in a writing group with my friends. They're not people I need to look pretty for. Which is why I'm very comfortable with them and not shy when we're together, but I suddenly had a big flare-up in my insecurities last week when two of the men in the group seemed to be treating one of my friends better than everyone else. She's a really popular girl anyway, which made me think, *Both of them must really like her. But why don't they like me? I must be really unattractive and hideous.* I felt so miserable that I was depressed that whole session. (Wow, this is painful for me to write. I really sound like a crazy person here.) I hated myself for thinking this way.

And another strange thing is, if I'm ever with a new group of people, I feel like I'll bounce off a wall if no one pays any attention to me. Instead of me waiting to see whether the men are any good, I feel like I'm waiting for them to make their judgements on my appearance. The funnier thing is that often I have no interest in the men but I'm hoping they're interested in me. Jesus, I really do hate myself, I'm pathetic.

Psychiatrist: When you're with an all-women group, do you talk about looks?

Me: I'm totally fine then.

Psychiatrist: Are you really?

Me: Actually, no, I'm not!

Psychiatrist: How do you feel when someone gets compliments and you don't?

Me: Oh, I get jealous, so jealous. Right, I'm like that with women as well. Which is why I get jealous of my colleagues at work.

Psychiatrist: Do you pay attention to your appearance in the morning when you're getting ready?

Me: Not really. Oh, I bet you don't have another patient as hopeless as me, doctor.

Psychiatrist: On the contrary.

Me: You do? I am so incredibly embarrassed right now. There are people who share thoughts as frivolous as these with you?

Psychiatrist: I imagine you are, but some people have a more roundabout way of getting to that point of embarrassment.

Me: Am I being very direct?

Psychiatrist: You are. Some talk about looks, others focus on it from the angle of other people's attention.

Me: Right. I really feel obsessive about my face and my charm. I really think I have no charm.

Psychiatrist: But you do have charm, otherwise you wouldn't have got any attention at all. But isn't the point more that you feel uncomfortable when you're pushed out of the spotlight slightly?

Me: Why am I doing this to myself? I don't *want* to be like this.

Psychiatrist: Have you heard of histrionic personality disorder? (A personality disorder where one exaggerates their expressions of emotion in order to draw attention to themselves.)

Me: No. Are you saying that's what I have?

Psychiatrist: I think you have a bit of a tendency towards it. You seek to be the centre of attention everywhere you go.

Me: Oh, yes, yes, yes, yes, that's exactly it.

Psychiatrist: There are usually two ways it manifests. One type might, in order to be more attractive, wear more revealing clothing or build muscle. The other, if they fail to be the centre of attention, tends to assume it's because people hate them and they berate themselves for it.

Me: I'm the latter, then.

Psychiatrist: The fact that you're aware of it suggests you're also aware that there's a lot of attention being paid to you. Most people don't realise it.

Me: I am very aware of it. I'm so sensitive to that sort of thing that every little word sounds like thunder. For example, at my writing group, I once went there in glasses instead of contact lenses, and the reaction was very positive. 'Hey, you're cuter in glasses! You should wear them all the time.' But that means if I don't wear glasses, I look ugly.

Psychiatrist: Okay, hang on – how did you get there all of a sudden?

Me: I'm being extreme again, aren't I. Anyway, I felt so insulted when they said that. And we took a group photo but one of the girls said I looked much prettier in person than in the photo. And she said to the boys, 'Doesn't she look much better in real life?' But they all said I looked the same. One of them even said I looked better in the photo. I was so annoyed with that.

Psychiatrist: Because you disagreed?

Me: Yes. I thought I looked weird in it . . . So I thought, well, maybe I'm just ugly.

Psychiatrist: That's a bit of an odd conclusion, don't you think?

Me: Right, I become ugly. Because I'm so extreme. I want to die.

Psychiatrist: And you keep this tendency of yours hidden?

Me: What do you mean by hidden?

Psychiatrist: You try to hide your obsession because you are aware of it, I mean.

Me: People say I'm very honest. But I thought to myself: *Am I really an honest person?* And I realised the part of me that I hide from all others is this part. Which is why I wanted to discuss it with you today. I always pretend it doesn't exist, and I keep it a secret.

Psychiatrist: It's difficult to admit to these things. The reason I said you had it hidden was because, remember that five-hundred-question survey I had you fill out at the very beginning of our sessions? It was a personality test. But there was no indication of this issue from the results, which is why I didn't expect to see it.

Me: What issue?

Psychiatrist: This obsession with your looks and the judgement from others. It doesn't show up on your tests. And I didn't pick up on it in our conversations.

Me: Then I've successfully kept it completely and utterly hidden?

Psychiatrist: Yes. (Laughs.) You are aware of the times when you're nervous about the possibility of people not saying you're pretty. This awareness is why, to use your expression, to not be pretty means you're 'just ugly'.

Me: Right. If I'm not liked, I immediately become a charmless, ugly person.

Psychiatrist: Isn't this something you've heard a lot before? Something rather familiar at this point?

Me: What something?

Psychiatrist: Your black-and-white extremism.

Me: Oh, that.

Psychiatrist: Everyone wants to be a star. Although there are occasionally people who want to play the supporting role. But the way you think leaves room only for the stars and the extras. The second you are not a star—

Me: I become one of the extras.

Psychiatrist: Yes. You think you'll be forgotten, and no one will know who you are.

Me: Wow. I really am very extreme. How did I get this way? (I feel like I keep asking this and hearing the same answers, then forgetting them.)

Psychiatrist: Well, it's hard to say it was one thing. Your perspective of yourself is so narrow and self-critical that you're unable to see things from a wider perspective, and so you goad yourself into choosing just one angle, which is the easiest way out.

Me: I don't quite understand that, but I'm going to try to be honest. And I'm going to write down my notes from today's session. What I honestly feel is that if my partner's friends don't think I'm pretty, my partner will stop seeing me through rose-coloured glasses.

Psychiatrist: Why, did you put a spell on them or something?

Me: No, it's just that everyone wears rose-coloured glasses in the beginning of a relationship.

Psychiatrist: Do you as well?

Me: Me too – oh, I see what you mean. That feeling doesn't change just because of someone else's judgement.

Psychiatrist: Let's go back to histrionic personality disorder.

Me: *Is* that what I have?

Psychiatrist: No, as I said you have some tendencies, but you don't quite fit the bill. However, you do have a fear of being pushed out of the spotlight. Being pushed out is fine, one can be a step or even two steps away from the spotlight, but you interpret any attempt to take the spotlight away from you as a large cane hooking you by the waist and dragging you off the stage. I think your fears are disproportionately large compared to the actual danger. It's a form of obsession.

Me: I'm very good at objectifying myself, you see. I know I'm not ugly. But I'm not pretty, either. I know I'm just ordinary, and I hate that even more.

Psychiatrist: Celebrities say the same thing.

Me: Like who?

Psychiatrist: You've heard that the ultra-handsome actor Jang Dong-gun once said, 'My face is really just ordinary'?

Me: Oh my god, that really is ridiculous.

Psychiatrist: It's perfectly understandable someone might think of themselves that way. What you said earlier could be a version of Jang Dong-gun saying he looks ordinary. If someone considers you very attractive, they might see this as an attempt at humility.

Me: How do I get out of this rut?

Psychiatrist: Do you think it can be forced?

Me: I wanted to avoid the looks-judging gaze, which is why I used to not do anything to my looks. No make-up, oversized clothing. Because then I don't get hurt and I can relax.

Psychiatrist: Were you paid attention when you did that?

Me: I don't think so.

Psychiatrist: No one said something like, 'You look pretty today'?

Me: Oh, wait, that did happen once.

Psychiatrist: Then how ugly, do you think, you have to force yourself into being?

Me: You're right. There was a time when I liked women more than men. Which was great because I could escape the male gaze. I liked girls so I didn't need to look good to men, and it didn't matter that men didn't like me. I think that was really comfortable for me, psychologically.

Psychiatrist: Just as you thought then, *I'm not ugly but I'm not pretty either*, you can also think something like, *I'm not this or that extreme, but in the scheme of things, I'm nice-looking.*

Me: I can?

Psychiatrist: And from that position you might go on to think, *This is where I am, and everyone has different standards, so some people will think I'm on one side and others will think I'm on the other.*

Me: Doctor, I really do practise that a lot. Because I know all too well. But when I'm thrown into a situation like with my partner yesterday, my mind goes blank.

Psychiatrist: Of course you feel pressured in a situation like that. Think about how pressured your partner would be if you'd gone around bragging about them as well. But the crux of the matter is that you keep believing you have to meet other people's expectations—

Me: (Practically about to rip my own hair out.) Oh my god, as if they even *have* expectations!

Who do I think is caring about me that much! I really am too ridiculous for words.

Psychiatrist: This is not a problem that you need to move on from, it's more of a question of enjoying your own appearance. Some days you'll feel like making an effort to look pretty, and on the days you don't feel that way you can just have an attitude that's like, 'Go ahead, judge all you want,' that kind of thing.

Me: And what about my wanting attention and the spotlight and everything?

Psychiatrist: You have a fear of losing attention, but I don't think you really want the attention itself. Because if you did, it would come out in your behaviour, as I previously mentioned. Dressing in revealing clothes or covering yourself in tattoos, that kind of thing.

Me: And you're saying I don't have any of those behaviours?

Psychiatrist: You don't. You only have a fear of being pushed out. We don't all wear pretty clothes every single day. Sometimes you'll leave the house with your hair a mess if you're just popping into the corner store. Some days you'll look pretty, and others you won't. It's a situation that can always change, so you don't have to keep thinking, *What are people* *going to say about me, what are they going to think?* Sometimes, you will disappoint people. You might think, *Aren't they interested in me anymore? Have their feelings changed?* But that shouldn't automatically make you think, *They hate me, I'm hideous.*

Me: I've thought in extremes for so long that I keep forgetting to think otherwise. You told me to change my attitude and create a middle ground for myself. You're asking me to apply that here as well, right?

Psychiatrist: There are so many ways to do it. And everyone is going to have a different perspective on you anyway.

Me: I really like faces that look the opposite of mine. I don't know if that's my taste or if I'm looking at it from a man's point of view.

Psychiatrist: Maybe because they have traits that you don't have.

Me: I want to love my own face, but I like other faces so much that I can't look pretty to myself. Sometimes I think I look pretty, but when people tell me I look pretty, I never agree with them.

Psychiatrist: The thing is, the people whose faces you like are probably beautiful, and the faces you don't like can be beautiful, too.

Me: So this is just me being extreme again.

Psychiatrist: It's your taste. The important thing is, you brought up the issue. The fact that you brought it up on your own is a significant act of courage, and now you can process it better.

Me: I do feel very relieved right now.

Psychiatrist: Fear increases when it's something that you keep to yourself. Instead of suffering alone, it can often be good to share it with someone else, like you're doing now. And if you don't want to see your partner's friends, you don't have to see them.

Me: I'm afraid of their judgement. I just really hate the prospect of them thinking I'm not pretty.

Psychiatrist: Wouldn't it be more of a relief if you just disappointed them up front and moved on?

Me: That's a good point.

Psychiatrist: Because if they go 'Wow, you're pretty!', you would have to keep making an effort not to disappoint them.

Me: Hmm . . . that's also true. Is this kind of stress why some women get plastic surgery?

Psychiatrist: It can be. A lot of people with histrionic personality disorder suffer from body dysmorphia. They keep thinking there's a problem with their looks. For example, that their reflections make them look twisted or crumpled.

Me: I think I have some of that!

Psychiatrist: (Chuckles.) No, I think you think that because you just heard me talking about it. I'm talking about something that's a kind of delusion, something people who suffer from this disorder actually see.

Me: Ah. I really hope it doesn't get that bad for me.

CONTRADICTORY ME

Even if I were fat or ugly, I want to acknowledge and love myself. But society teaches us to judge each other's weight, and my father and older sister would praise me whenever I happened to lose a few pounds. I don't think I look healthier or feel better when I'm thinner, but I do think I have more confidence.

I thought about whether this confidence was because I believed being thin might lead to better health, but I don't think that's it; it's because I feel more in control. I hate thinking I'm getting ugly, or not wearing what I want. Which is why I become obsessed with my weight. The social gaze is so insidious, and despite any escape being impossible, I want to escape it. But I don't want to deliberately become fat, either.

I don't know why an individual has to be treated as less-than and strive to fit society's standards when it's the people who denigrate others who are the real problem. That frustrates me. That I can't step out of this frame, that I still feel inferior when I meet someone supposedly superior to me, and that I feel confident and comfortable when I meet someone supposedly inferior – I absolutely loathe that about myself.

10

WHY DO YOU LIKE ME? WILL YOU STILL LIKE ME IF I DO THIS? OR THIS?

I took a self-esteem quiz on the Internet and scored a -22. I knew I had low self-esteem, and I think this was actually a higher score than one I received a few years ago, which was why I joked to my friend and family about it, but I didn't really feel that good. My anxiety towards new situations and how I appear to others, and how this comes out as hostility towards others – these were all problems so entrenched that it seemed hopeless to try to solve them. Which in turn made me upset and sad. It was impossible for me to imagine feeling warmth or comfort from most people. I also didn't know how to not blame myself for weaknesses or faults.

Psychiatrist: How have you been? Did you meet your partner's friends?

Me: No. I didn't. My partner read something I wrote about my obsession with looks and they were surprised. They said they had no idea I was under such pressure. That if I didn't want to meet their friends, I didn't have to. But I did feel relief when I told them, and a bit of embarrassment as well.

Psychiatrist: Of course you did. You've revealed feelings you've kept hidden for decades, of course you're going to feel embarrassed. Think of it as a transitional phase.

Me: I thought I was fairly candid, but it turns out, I've got a lot of things I keep hidden. For example, my partner was reading my writing out loud in front of me. That was so embarrassing, I hated it, but then I thought, *No, don't hate it, accept it.* But my immediate feelings in that moment had been, *Oh, no, I hate it that it's being read aloud.* Which is why I decided to go with my first feeling and say, 'Please don't read it out loud.' These days I don't put myself through layers of censorship, I try to say what I feel in the moment.

Psychiatrist: That sounds like it could become a bit compulsive.

Me: You're right. And I'm trying to fix my habit of thinking in extremes. I have a friend I'm close to at work, and we often talk about difficulties we're having. But I happened to be really busy and not in the right frame of mind for it, and my friend was suddenly pouring her heart out. That was hard for me. Normally my brain would process it as, *Wow, she must really look down on me if she thinks she can dump all of this on me, am I her emotional waste bin?* And I'd get all whipped up in my own emotions, you know? *I'm such a doormat, such a stupid girl.* But this time I thought, *I must be a really comforting presence to her, which is why she's telling me these things, it's not because she looks down on me.*

Psychiatrist: I think you can tweak that a bit further even.

Me: How?

Psychiatrist: You might think, *She really must not have anyone else who can help her talk about these feelings.*

Me: But that would be so presumptuous of me!

Psychiatrist: I'm only saying you should enjoy the freedom of your own thoughts.

Me: I see. Which reminds me, nowadays I keep thinking the phrase, *That goddamn self-esteem.* Like, why is it such a big deal to have that goddamn self-esteem? But in books, we're always being told that we have to love ourselves if we want to love others, that if we denigrate ourselves, others will denigrate us as well. I tended to think that was nonsense. I've hated myself for such a long time. But there have always been people who love me! And I don't love myself, but I do love others. Does that love have anything to do with self-esteem?

Psychiatrist: Those books mean that you might have a warped perspective of love if you don't love yourself.

Me: Warped perspective?

Psychiatrist: Yes, because you'll begin to suspect the love you receive. For example, if you don't like your looks but someone else gives you a compliment, you might think, *Why is he doing that to me? Does he have bad intentions?* On the other hand, if you are satisfied with your looks, you can simply accept the compliment as is. The important thing here isn't whether you are being loved, it's how you will accept the love that comes your way.

Me: I see . . . It's a question of acceptance. You're saying if I had self-esteem, my thoughts would flow in a more positive and healthy direction?

Psychiatrist: Let's take as an example that someone loves you. There's a clear difference between thinking, *I like certain aspects of me, too, maybe I should give him a chance?* and thinking, *Why would he like someone like me? Is he weird?*

Me: Oh . . . you're right.

Psychiatrist: Your self-esteem determines how you feel about the sincerity of others. In truth, there really are no sure-fire ways to increase your self-esteem. But what you mentioned doing earlier, how it occurred to you that you would've reacted differently before to certain situations – an awareness of that is in itself a great start. Because being aware of something is a huge step in the right direction.

Me: I had no idea I was so extreme in my thoughts. Other people might mention that about me, but I'd only think, *It's because you don't know me very well.*

Psychiatrist: Extreme thinking can go in different directions. There are those who put themselves down all the time and those who puff themselves up all the time. If both of these people were searching for a middle ground, wouldn't the person who puts themselves down be more likely to succeed than the person who loves themselves too much?

Me: Is it really harder for people who love themselves too much?

Psychiatrist: In that they don't feel a need for treatment. And they refuse to listen to others because it lowers their fun and confidence. There are people who come here basically asking for validation, wanting me to tell them they're great. They think that people are jealous of them.

Me: It must be difficult for such people to get better. They'd interpret any criticism as jealousy.

Psychiatrist: They have subconsciously constructed a new persona in order to conquer their low self-esteem, or they cover up their hated bits and play up the opposite of what they are. They pretend they have high self-esteem, but they get wounded more easily that way.

Me: I see.

Psychiatrist: A common symptom of delusions of grandeur is mania. It happens as a defence against very acute depression. They might seem their usual selves one day and then make you think, 'This person is crazy!' the next – usually that means it's a manic episode. When schizophrenia progresses slowly, manic states begin popping up at random moments. A more serious manifestation of this results in claims like, 'I am Jesus, I am Buddha.' And sometimes they think someone is out to get them, and they go into hiding.

Me: That sounds really awful for them. (Why are we talking about manic states now . . . ?)

Psychiatrist: The episodes are not long. And once they're back to their usual selves, they can feel really bad.

Me: Are they trying to escape from a stressful reality?

Psychiatrist: That's it. The pious ones who go to church several times a week suddenly become a god. Thinking they can save others.

Me: Oh . . . Actually, I have a new worry. (Seeing as I changed the subject here, I must not have been very interested in the topic.)

Psychiatrist: What is it?

Me: I don't want to drink as much as I do. My eczema flares up when I do. I drank too much last night and my skin looked terrible this morning, and I feel so guilty.

Psychiatrist: When did you first start thinking you should drink less?

Me: I've always had that thought. But in the evenings after I come home, it's become almost a ritual for me.

Psychiatrist: What is it about drinking that helps you?

Me: I like the dreamy state I get into.

Psychiatrist: Does your mind feel more at ease then?

Me: Yes. My mind feels more at ease, and I can write better.

Psychiatrist: You might say it's a tool for your writing?

Me: Maybe a little bit. (There are times when I drink so I can write better, but to be honest, that's just a small part of it.)

Psychiatrist: It's not as if you become completely drunk in order to write?

Me: I don't. If I get that drunk, forget writing, I turn into a puddle. I drink without restraint, until I am completely and utterly drunk.

Psychiatrist: Even when you're drinking alone?

Me: Sometimes, but especially when I drink with a friend who likes to drink, I can't control myself.

Psychiatrist: Then don't meet that friend.

Me: That's true. Do you have patients who come to you because they want to stop drinking?

Psychiatrist: I do.

Me: What methods do you recommend them?

Psychiatrist: If they're so dependent on alcohol that they feel discomfort not drinking for just a day, then I recommend they check themselves into a facility. If it's not that serious, I prescribe medication that lowers compulsive feelings.

Me: I'd like to try that medication.

Psychiatrist: Your drinking is for the sake of feeling more at ease. Do you have withdrawal symptoms when you wake up? Sometimes, we use medication that mitigates withdrawal symptoms. They work by giving you the same feeling of ease.

Me: Am I not serious enough to warrant pills? I do like the taste of alcoholic drinks.

Psychiatrist: I don't think you warrant them. Are you trying to quit altogether?

Me: No. I like drinking too much.

Psychiatrist: You just want to drink in moderation, correct?

Me: Yes. And drinking makes me gain weight. I want to drink only on the weekends, but I can't get myself to stick to that plan.

Psychiatrist: Drinking out of habit and drinking because you feel you really need to are two different things. I think you need to apply your willpower. If that doesn't work, we could move on to trying pills. Try strategising your drinking, like limiting the days you meet with drinking friends.

Me: All right . . .

LIFE

'The important thing here isn't whether you are being loved, it's how you will accept the love that comes your way.'

I've come to an awareness of my black-and-white worldview and I'm trying to change the direction of my thoughts. I still have the most extreme thoughts when it comes to the relationship that has the lion's share of my fears – my romantic relationship – but I have hopes that I will improve.

I still drink, and because of my grandmother's eightieth birthday celebrations and my cousin's wedding, I could not come to therapy for the next two weeks. Maybe that was the reason I started getting headaches, would burst into tears for no reason and felt unstable and emotionally exhausted.

The Lee Young-hak incident[1] and other social problems that came up around then made me feel weaker as well. I also became much more sensitive; I wanted to shout at the middle-aged men who walked down crowded sidewalks, smoking their cigarettes without any consideration for others. Over a period of thirty minutes I saw seven smokers, and they were all middle-aged men. Hate them. Hate them. Hate them.

---

[1] Translator's note: A heavily reported case in 2017 of the sexual assault and murder of a minor.

11

I DON'T LOOK PRETTY

Psychiatrist: How have you been?

Me: I think I've been all right, but something has happened. The company Instagram account I used to run has gone over to another team, and seeing their first posts made me feel sad. I feel like the new person in charge of it does a better job than I did, that the company will be fine even if I disappeared, and the thought that my place in the company was shrinking made me feel down. I think I'm afraid of competition.

Psychiatrist: Do you think that's competition?

Me: Isn't it?

Psychiatrist: You're feeling like you're not part of that team anymore?

Me: Right. I'm anxious that I've lost my place.

Psychiatrist: But that's just your perspective. Just like how the grass always looks greener on the other side, don't you think you're taking for granted all the things that you're actually very good at? I think you should accept that you have your strong points as well.

Me: Right. I never accept that, I just criticise myself. When I read books, I only look back at how ignorant I was and scold myself and feel bad about being so stupid.

Psychiatrist: Is there anything about yourself that you accept as good?

Me: (I think for a long time.)

Psychiatrist: Or any part of you that you don't criticise yourself for?

Me: I don't judge people for how much or little money they have. And I read a novel recently that's written from the perspective of a mother who has a lesbian daughter, and in it the mother thinks her daughter is abnormal and the world is ending because her daughter is gay. Maybe some readers will agree with the mother, but I didn't think her daughter was abnormal at all.

Psychiatrist: You have sympathy for social minorities. Perhaps that comes from seeing yourself as disadvantaged?

Me: I don't think I'm particularly sympathetic—

Psychiatrist: Or you're able to empathise with them.

Me: Well, I see them as minorities.

Psychiatrist: Yes. But you yourself try to fit into a frame, as if you were under great pressure to conform, to prevent yourself from being seen as abnormal.

Me: I do do that. And I'm still experiencing side effects.

Psychiatrist: Like what?

Me: Last night, I took some pills and fell asleep, but I woke up at dawn. My heart was racing and I was so nervous and (I burst into tears) I was crying like this. You know how my survey said I was 'faking bad' (tendency to see oneself as worse off than one actually is). Which is why I kept telling myself, *You're overreacting, things aren't that bad.* But I just felt it was so unfair to be thinking that. I wanted to prove how bad things were. So I took some emergency pills and a sleeping pill and just passed out into sleep.

Psychiatrist: Faking bad can be a function of cognitive distortion. To use your work as an example, it's when you think your company can function perfectly well without you when you're actually a crucial part of operations there. You become so immersed in bad feelings that they take over your mind.

Me: I don't know how long it will take for me to shake it. It's all so hard. I'm so happy when I manage to change course in my thoughts, but I've had so many years of thinking negatively that it's not easy.

Psychiatrist: I want you to try doing something you've never done before. I don't think your current methods for getting away from depressive or empty thoughts are very effective. Maybe you need to do something more dramatic.

Me: You want me to go rogue?

Psychiatrist: What would going rogue mean for you?

Me: Quitting my job.

Psychiatrist: I see.

Me: That's right. That would be the end of it. And I gained five kilos since the summer.

Psychiatrist: Really? You don't look like you have. Was there a particular reason?

Me: I just ate food I like and drank a lot.

Psychiatrist: But you said you drank a lot before.

Me: That's right. I think when people look at me it's because I've gained weight, and they think I'm fat.

Psychiatrist: Do you feel that way when you look at yourself in the mirror?

Me: Yes. I'm too plump. I want to be happy when I'm plump, but that's not easy.

Psychiatrist: Do you think you can be happy being plump in your current emotional state?

Me: I just think people will mock me or humiliate me.

Psychiatrist: You said you want to be happy even if you're plump but it's not like you mock people you think are overweight, do you?

Me: I judge them.

Psychiatrist: As people who can't effectively manage themselves?

Me: They just don't look attractive. I don't like men who are on the heavy side, either.

Psychiatrist: I wonder if it's an effect of the medicine. It doesn't necessarily make you gain weight, but it does bring back your appetite.

Me: Are you going to try to wean me off of them eventually?

Psychiatrist: It depends, but your wishes are the most important in this.

Me: If I don't take the pills, I feel terrible. I like not being depressed. But I feel like I've exchanged my depression for these side effects.

Psychiatrist: Side effects can be a matter of adjustment.

Me: Then adjust me already!

Psychiatrist: We will. We don't want you to feel uncomfortable. But you said your life was difficult now? This feeling that the ground beneath your feet is giving way. My hope is for you to think of the medication as, *I have this to help me through it.*

Me: Fine. But why do I have sudden headaches?

Psychiatrist: You might get headaches from the pills.

Me: Another thing: I've been reading a book called *Humiliation**, and I realise I feel humiliation really easily. I think I try so hard

---

* Translator's note: *Humiliation* (모멸감) by Kim Chan-ho, a critical essay on the nature of humiliation in Korean society.

to be nice to others because of it. I remember staying at a guesthouse once. The first person I shared a room with was really nice, but the person I met on the second day seemed to be looking down on me a bit. It hurt my feelings. I realised, having read the *Humiliation* book, that I interpreted the person's attitude negatively because I have low self-esteem. The person could've simply been tired, but I took it as, *She's looking down on me!* It meant a lot for me to realise this.

Psychiatrist: I don't think you need to find the reason for everything in yourself. You could've just been having a bad day.

How are things with your older sister?

Me: Oh right, she seems to have changed. She used to treat me like I was beneath her, but now she seems to see me as an equal. She even asked me to buy her a nice dress, and came to me for advice.

Psychiatrist: What do you feel about her doing this?

Me: I don't really think about her. In the past, I would blame everything on her and be so angry with her, but I don't do that anymore.

Psychiatrist: I think you also lower yourself in order to elevate others. When comparing yourself to your colleagues at work, you only see in them what you don't have. You praise them and criticise yourself.

Me: But I'm also two-faced, because I look down on others in silence. And I exclude them.

Psychiatrist: Yes. But again, you can enjoy the freedom of your own thoughts. Instead of thinking, *I must not have these thoughts.*

FREE DEATH

'You're overreacting, things are not that bad. But I just felt it was so unfair to be thinking that. I wanted to prove how bad things were.'

In Hong Seung-hee's *Suicide Diaries*[*], I read about her thoughts on free death. In the same way the Korean word for menopause should not be 'menstrual shutdown' but 'menstrual completion', she thought that the word 'suicide' should be replaced with 'free death', a linguistic idea that made an impression on me. There are so many words with highly negative meanings, textures and impressions: abortion, menopause, suicide and so on.

It's impossible to fathom the sadness of those who are left behind, but if life gives one more suffering than death, shouldn't we respect their right to end life? We are so bad at mourning in our society. Maybe it's a failure of respect. Some call those who choose their own death sinners or failures or losers who give up. Is living until the end really a triumph in every case? As if there can be any true winning or losing in this game of life.

*

---

[*] Translator's note: A column on depression and suicide. Ran in the now-defunct publication *Newdam* in late 2017.

I think I'm going to quit my job. Life is all about getting better and getting worse and getting better again, so getting worse is a natural part of life and I just have to learn to deal with it.

12

ROCK BOTTOM

I feel completely drained. I don't want to work. During a work lunch, I wasn't particularly trying to get attention but I found it hard to sympathise with my colleagues, which depressed me a little. Some people said a friend of mine was very pretty and that made me jealous. And it made me dislike her. I'm so horrible.

Am I really a warm person? I don't think of myself as a good person, to be honest. I just don't want my sensitivity and anxiety to be embarrassing to others, that's all.

Psychiatrist: Did you have a good week?

Me: No. I most certainly did not.

Psychiatrist: What happened?

Me: Depressed and drained. No motivation at work. I told them last week I was quitting. My boss asked me why, and I told her it was because of mental and physical reasons. I said I was getting treatment, and she understood. And she told me my quitting this way could increase my anxiety. And that I should take the next week off and we could talk about giving me more freedom in my role when I got back in November. And that if I still felt the same way, we could revisit the matter then.

Psychiatrist: How did that make you feel?

Me: So grateful that I almost cried. I worked there for four years without a break. You know the sense of stability a company can bring into your life (regular schedules, the salary and so on). I was afraid of leaving that stability behind, but tabling my resignation made me feel relieved. But I did think it was going to be temporary. My state of mind in the office is always the same. I'm so bored, and I feel like I'm just living from day to day. I don't know how things got this way. It's been like this for two months. Oh, and I'm taking a trip to Gyeongju tomorrow, alone.

Psychiatrist: How do you usually feel after the work day is over?

Me: I have no energy. The only fun I have is walking home from work at the end of the day, and I just feel so listless when I'm home. As soon as I think, *Should I do something?*, I immediately think, *I don't want to do anything at all.*

Psychiatrist: So what do you end up doing?

Me: Binge eating. Biscuits and chocolates and alcohol. All the while stressing out at the prospect of gaining weight. Everything is a mess.

Psychiatrist: How are things with your partner?

Me: That's the only good thing in my life right now. The only moment where things feel calm. They try their best to tolerate me and be there for me, which makes me lean on them a lot.

Psychiatrist: Do you think you'll get tired of that dynamic once you get used to it?

Me: It's fine for now, I don't know about the future.

Psychiatrist: Did something happen?

Me: You know how I handle social media in our company? I used to plan all of our online content. But because I can't do everything on my own, the planning and marketing teams started participating in the content development. Which was fine at first, but as the processes were set up, I became someone who just posts the content online. I suppose I could make more content on my own, but I have no motivation to do it. I feel like my position in the company is shrinking.

Psychiatrist: What was it like when you were completely in charge? Did you get good results?

Me: I did. I had lots of fun and got good results. My boss said I should think about commissioning a book and do something fun, and I'm so grateful to her for suggesting that, but nowadays I'm just wallowing in the thought of, *What on earth am I doing here?*

Psychiatrist: Have you thought of what you might do after you quit?

Me: I'm writing a book. I want to finish that, and start my own business. With my compensation package, and some part-time work. Once my business takes off, I'm going to change jobs.

Psychiatrist: Do you feel motivated in your writing?

Me: I am. I've written a lot of the book, and I'll be finished around spring.

Psychiatrist: I wonder if your boss is right and you're just exhausted. You don't seem drained and listless in other areas of your life. Don't you think your trip will help you recharge?

Me: I don't know. I recharged a lot during the Chuseok holidays. I feel like I'll go crazy because I'm so unmotivated. I keep getting angry all the time and my mind is in tatters.

Psychiatrist: Even if the changes in season don't bother you normally, this is that time of year where depression increases. The way in which you rest is also important. I hope you take in lots of sunlight and walk as much as you can on your trip.

Me: I will. I just want to shake off this tedium.

Psychiatrist: Why did you choose to go alone on this trip?

Me: If I go with someone else, I have to compromise on the things we can do together, but I figured if I went alone, I would get to choose whatever I wanted to do.

Psychiatrist: Good idea. I think it's something you really need right now, to spend time alone. Why did you pick Gyeongju?

Me: I didn't know where to go and I had no motivation. A friend of mine happened to send me pictures of her Gyeongju trip, and the old temples and buildings looked peaceful, which I really liked. I wanted to walk among them.

Psychiatrist: I think it's good to experience complete solitude in an unfamiliar environment. You're not hitting rock bottom right now. When we're sinking in water, it can be a relief to feel the ground beneath our feet, the rock bottom, because we know we can kick against it to rise again. But if you can't feel the ground in life, the fear can be overwhelming. So maybe it's good to find your rock bottom.

Me: What would that feel like for me?

Psychiatrist: It would be to feel an even bigger devastation and loneliness than you do now. I'm going to change your medication a bit. The antidepressants will lift you from the ground a little more, and I'll also include some mood stabilisers. How is your concentration?

Me: It sort of comes and goes, all at once.

Psychiatrist: Do you cry a lot these days?

Me: Last Monday when I went to get my medications I cried a lot, and cried yesterday – I guess about three times this week.

Psychiatrist: I think what you're describing is a bit different from regular depression. There's a kind of ADHD that manifests in adults. The symptoms include feelings of emptiness, boredom and a decrease in concentration. I'll prescribe something for that as well.

Me: (I feel like this describes my mood perfectly.) Yes, thank you.

Psychiatrist: In any case, enjoy your trip, and the next time we meet, I hope you tell me more about your older sister and parents, whom we keep putting off talking about.

Me: I will.

13

EPILOGUE: IT'S OKAY, THOSE WHO DON'T FACE DARKNESS CAN NEVER APPRECIATE THE LIGHT

I tended to discount anything positive that happened to fall into my hands. Even when I managed to accomplish something difficult, or when I wore a pretty dress, I would immediately decide my accomplishment was no big deal; the dress would lose its power. Nothing in my grasp seemed precious or beautiful. The real problem was how this principle began to apply to people as well. The more someone loved me, the more I got bored of them. Perhaps not bored – they ceased to sparkle in my eyes.

The problem is, of course, my self-esteem. I look down on myself so much that I try to gain self-validation through the eyes of others. But because that's not a validation that I am able to accept, there's a limit to how satisfying it can be, and I become bored of it. Which is why I go looking for someone else, and ultimately why I think someone liking me cannot in itself satisfy me. I'm devastated if someone I like doesn't like me, and devastated when someone does end up loving me; either way, I am looking at myself through the eyes of another. In the end, I'm torturing myself.

It was also revealed that the reason I am cruel to others is because I have low-self-esteem. Because I don't love myself, I am unable to understand those who do love me in spite of it all, and so I test them. 'You love me even when I do this? Or this? Or this?' Even when the other person forgives me, I am unable to understand their forgiveness, and when they give up on me, I torture and console myself with the 'fact' that no one could ever love me.

That goddamn self-esteem. I don't want any more twisted relationships, and I'm tired of not being able to find satisfaction in the present and being obsessed with the past or having high expectations of new relationships. But if this is because of low self-esteem, I don't know which direction I should move in. I have come to a point where I am no longer able to tell the difference between my loving someone and not loving someone. I am so tired of myself for being lost in the woods all the time with no plan of action, for having so little willpower and being so wishy-washy.

My psychiatrist apologised to me for not presenting a master method or answer. But just as a person who is dropped into a dark well must make a circle in order to determine they are inside a well, I am sure my continued attempts to be better will take shape into something resembling an octagon, or even a dodecahedron, and maybe one day a circle. I was told that my accumulated mistakes will create a stronger sense of self, that I was doing just fine, that I was perfectly capable of looking at the other side of the coin, but the coin just happens to be a little heavy, that's all.

What do I wish for? I want to love and be loved. Without suspicion, and with ease. That's it. I don't know how to love or be loved properly, and that's what pains me. After transcribing my last session, I went for a long time not being able to write an epilogue. I think I wanted to show how much I'd improved, I wanted some kind of grand finale. I thought that was the proper way to end a book.

But even as I read my finished manuscript, I still hate the way I go in and out of depression and happiness, and it's hard to find meaning in it. I went in and out of the clinic that way, and here I am, before I realised it, years later.

Looking more closely at myself, there are parts that I've improved on. My depression has lessened a lot, and so has my anxiety over my relationships. But other problems have filled the cracks, and the culprit that thwarted every effort I made in exploring my problems in detail was my self-esteem. Because I still remain someone who is unable to love herself.

But as I had that thought, I had another: light and darkness are part of the same thing. Happiness and unhappiness alternate throughout life, as in a dance. So as long as I keep going and don't give up, surely I will keep having moments of tears and laughter.

This book, therefore, ends not with answers but with a wish. I want to love and be loved. I want to find a way where I don't hurt myself. I want to live a life where I say things are good more than things are bad. I want to keep failing and discovering new and better directions. I want to enjoy the tides of feeling in me as the rhythms of life. I want to be the kind of person who can walk inside the vast darkness and find the one fragment of sunlight I can linger in for a long time.

Some day, I will.

14

PSYCHIATRIST'S NOTE: FROM ONE INCOMPLETENESS TO ANOTHER

I still remember when the author turned on her recording device. She said she was having trouble remembering what we had discussed once she got home and asked for my consent to record our sessions. I gave it without much thought, but I did find myself choosing my words more carefully, knowing that my words as a therapist were being recorded. Then the author told me she was creating a book from our therapy sessions and was sending me the manuscript. I felt naked and worried about what others would think, which made me reluctant to turn the first page. I read the book only when it was published, and I was even more embarrassed than I had expected to be as I regretted some of my counselling choices and wished I could've been a bigger help to the author.

On the other hand, the author's writing in the book gave off a much more vivid energy than the dry sentences I recorded in her patient chart. Finding facts and information about the terms in this book – depression, anxiety, dysthymia and so on – isn't too hard in today's society. But for a patient to brave societal prejudices and reveal in such vivid detail all the experiences that led her to seek treatment and the difficult process of treatment itself – this is perhaps not something that is as easily googleable as the name of an antidepressant.

This is a record of a very ordinary, incomplete person who meets another very ordinary, incomplete person, the latter of whom happens to be a therapist. The therapist makes some mistakes and has a bit of room for improvement, but life has always been like that, which means everyone's life – our readers included – has the potential to become better. To our readers, who are perhaps down and out from having experienced much devastation or are living day-to-day in barely contained anxiety: I hope you will listen to a certain overlooked and different voice within you. Because the human heart, even when it wants to die, quite often wants at the same time to eat some tteokbokki, too.

15

POSTSCRIPT: REFLECTIONS ON LIFE
FOLLOWING THERAPY

THE POISON OF CHEER

My mother always thought of herself as having no confidence and being stupid. Her sentences often contained self-castigation. 'I'm terrible with directions, I'm stupid, I don't understand other people when they talk, I have no confidence, I can't do anything.'

There was no way we wouldn't take after her to some extent. My sisters and I are clearly more introverted than extroverted, and we all have low self-esteem. It was much worse when we were little, and the three of us were very easily frightened and intimidated as children. Mother would always point out our faults no matter whom she was talking to: 'This one has no confidence, she has eczema.'

Naturally my shame was instilled early. As I grew up, I longed to be confident and to exude attitude. I didn't want to be intimidated anymore. When I asked my mother, 'Why do I have so little confidence?' she answered, 'What do you mean? Stop that! Be confident!' I scoffed at that. Mother clearly hated how she had passed on this part of herself to us, which was why she was always angry at our faults. She had wanted us to be talented but we hadn't any talent; she wanted us to be good public speakers but we weren't. She wanted us to do what she had wanted to do, like become a flight attendant or take up jazz dancing. I'm grateful she wasn't one to force such things on us.

At some point, people telling me to cheer up or be confident or not be intimidated began to really make me angry. I was always an introvert and a shrinking violet, and often got into trouble for it at school or work. Group projects and meetings made my flesh crawl. As soon as I'd start to think of myself as experienced and prepared, I'd run into more obstacles – new people, new work, new topics and new places. Like a game where no matter how many walls you break, there's another wall waiting for you on the other side.

Funnily enough, the most consoling words I'd ever heard were these: 'Why are you trying to be brave? Why are you trying to be confident? Just go ahead and feel what you feel. Don't cheer up!'

If I try to disguise myself as something I am not, I'm only going to get caught in the act eventually. And I hate my awkward posing, my pretending to be something I am not. And there's nothing more awkward than a person who isn't daring pretending to be daring (of course, pretending to be daring and trying to be daring are different things). What terrible advice to offer a person with no confidence: to pretend to have confidence. What could be more misguided than telling a fearful person not to fear? What could be more pathetic than a weak person pretending to be stronger than they are?

Which is why when I had to do presentations in college, I always warned my class. 'I get so nervous during presentations that my face turns red. My nickname during high school was the Red Human. If you happen to see my face turning as red as a tomato, please don't be alarmed.' The students would laugh. And surprisingly enough, I could get through the presentation without my face turning red.

Sometimes, when someone tells me to 'Cheer up' when I'm going through a tough time, I just want to wring their neck. Just be there to hold my hand, be sad or angry with me, or if you've gone through something similar, tell me about it and say it will all pass eventually. That's empathy and communication and a kind of consolation that enriches relationships.

Today I am meeting the author of the first book I'd ever commissioned. I've never done anything like this before, and I have to explain to them what kind of book I want them to write and how we are going to go about it. I have to be careful and yet natural, as this is work between two people. I will be under my boss's watchful eye. Normally I'm very intimidated and have low confidence, but I don't want to have to hide that about me. I'm not going to emphasise it or anything but I'm not going to thrust my chest out and talk in a loud voice, pretending I'm someone I'm not, either. I'm just going to be as honest as possible. It's my first time doing this, there's no way to do it perfectly, anyway. I have to remind myself of that and think of ways to do it better next time. I also have to comfort myself, tell myself it's all right; I don't have to 'cheer up'.

Sometimes, this directive to cheer up and buck up is like poison that rots one's soul. Note that the bestselling self-help books and essay collections of the past ten years aren't about whipping yourself, they're about healing and consolation. Being imperfect is all right and being awkward is okay. You don't have to cheer up. I can do well today, or not. It'll be an experience either way. And that's fine.

TURNING MY GAZE

Whenever my self-consciousness hits overflow, or I feel weighed down by anxiety, sadness, irritation or fear, I think to myself: I have to turn my gaze.

I think I've realised that this constant internal fighting is never going to make me feel better about myself. And how exhausting it is to have the whole world's motivations and intentions bearing down on my shoulders!

So I turn my gaze. From despair to hope. From discomfort to comfort. From the majority to the minority. From the things that are useful but make me rust to the things that are useless but make me beautiful.

Once I turn my gaze, I see the more interesting aspects of life. And my gaze guides my behaviour. And my behaviour changes my life. I realise that I can't change all by myself; what makes me really change are the myriad things of the universe that my gaze happens to rest upon. Through turning my gaze, I learn that the low points of life can be filled with countless realisations.

My head is full of good writing I've come across, but it's hard to find good people. It's because becoming a good person (my ideal of what I should be) is a very difficult process. Aside from characteristics one happens to be born with, it's hard to change all the thoughts and attitudes that have accumulated over the years. Which is why even after coming across a piece of advice and realising how good it is, I can't follow it for more than three days. Words and behaviours are very different, and while hiding words is easy, hiding the behaviour that reaches out from one's subconscious is impossible.

Most people have trouble living a life where their words match their actions. No matter how much they read and try to remember, they always return to their old patterns. I admire those who realise their past mistakes and prove how they've changed through their behaviour.

Perhaps this is why we feel discomfort when reading the words of those who are always *saying* the right things. Because it's so rare to see someone who walks the talk. The silly thing is, we feel uncomfortable even if we do find someone who walks the talk. We feel smaller next to them, afraid that they will see us for what we are and look down on us. Maybe this is why I feel more comfortable with people who are unpretentious and uncomplicated.

I am in a vague state at the moment, which is not good. I was born depressed and pathetic. I don't have deep thoughts or powers of insight. The only things I'm good at are regret and self-criticism, and even these I can only pause, never stop completely. I understand all this with my brain, but I have the hardest time modifying my behaviour appropriately. I support feminism and rail against racism, but I find myself shrinking away from a passing foreigner or my body reacts with distaste at the sight of a lesbian who doesn't put on make-up for valid political reasons. My hypocrisy disgusts me.

But nothing comes from scolding myself or hating myself for these feelings. I simply must accept that I have room for improvement, and consider these moments as constant opportunities for self-reflection, to feel shame and joy at having learned something new and to keep inching towards change.

I can't suddenly become like the people I envy. That would be truly impossible. The only way for me to become a better person is to go my way little by little, as tedious as that can be. To delay my judgement, to not force myself, to accept the countless judgements and emotions that pass through me. Criticising myself isn't going to make me a cleverer person suddenly.

I think I am learning how to accept life as it is. Accepting your burdens and putting them down isn't an occasional posture; it's something you need to practise for the rest of your life. To see the pathetic little me as I am, but also to see that the pathetic other person I am relating to is trying their best. Instead of ruthlessly judging others the way I judge myself or trying to bend others to fit my rules.

I've got to accept that everyone has a flaw or two, and first and foremost, see myself as I am first. I must stop expecting myself to be perfect. The best I can do is to learn or realise something new every day.

THE QUESTION OF LOVE

Looking back, I seem to have made a lot of decisions based on love. There were moments where I would refrain from calculating the gains and losses and simply choose what my heart told me to. I used my rationality in school and work only. In those spheres my first considerations were pride and money, which I prioritised over my dreams and my writing, because sometimes life makes even choosing the second-most important thing an impossibility.

That's how it is with the people I love. I love the light in their eyes, their passion and their courage in leaping into love. I've never loved anyone with half of my heart thinking, this is enough for me. As passive as I am, I share my everything. Perhaps I am bad at making detailed plans or am unable to imagine a neat future because of these tendencies.

Meeting someone who moves your heart, writing something until it moves the hearts of others, listening to music and watching movies that depict love – I want to always be motivated by love. If pure rationality keeps forcing itself into the spaces in between, I shall lose the shine and comfort of my life – which is why I want to be an emotionally bright person, even if it means becoming impoverished in terms of rationality. I want to hold hands and march with those who feel similarly to me. It's difficult to say whether sense or sensibility is the superior of the two, but they definitely have different textures. And the texture I enjoy more of the two is definitely one of love and sensibility.

SOLITUDE IS A VERY SPECIAL PLACE

There are eyes on the walls. And inside the phones of strangers, on the partitions in offices, in the air that sweeps through the streets. Once solitude opens its eyes, the face of fear begins showing itself, and countless eyes blink in the dark as they scrutinise my words and expressions.

To me, solitude is my one-bedroom apartment, underneath the blanket that fits me perfectly, beneath the sky I find myself staring at while out on a walk, a feeling of alienation that comes over me in the middle of a party. It's in my self-criticism, in moments when my hands fidget in my pockets, in the emptiness of my room after I've played back my voice on the recorder, when I've accidently met eyes with someone staring off into space in a café – when despite my fear of the gaze of others, I find that no one is looking in the first place. Can all the solitude I've drawn from these places become something special? This is the task and privilege of all artists.

Ruminating on love, work or anything really, I often have thoughts like *Ah, I was wrong about that, I should've known better,* and this both pains and consoles me at the same time. I am pained by the thought that I could never go back and correct it, and consoled by the thought that I won't make the same mistake again. If the incident has to do with work the consolation is bigger, but with love, it's the pain that looms larger. Because the moment I realise I should do better comes just when the person I should do better with is no longer by my side.

It's no use to hold on to the empty shell of a love that's past, to try to win back a heart that will never return, or to let your regrets eat you up from the inside . . .

On those days, I read. Because there really is no torture greater than endlessly rambling on about unshakeable feelings for another person. That just results in cycles of meaningless emotional consumption, for myself and for whomever is listening. But books are different. I often look for books that are like medicine, that fit my situation and my thoughts, and I read them over and over again until the pages are tattered, underlining everything, and still the book will have something to give me. Books never tire of me. And in time they present a solution, quietly waiting until I am fully healed. That's one of the nicest things about books.

A LIFE WITH NO MODIFIERS

A new book by a favourite writer is being published very soon by the company I work for. The editor in charge set a brainstorming session with the author for mid-February and asked me to attend if I could, adding that she knew the author was a favourite, and encouraging me, as a young twenty-something, to present as many fresh ideas as possible.

The prospect of attending the meeting excited me, but hearing myself being called 'young' made my heart catch in my throat. I was nervous; how was I to present fresh ideas that no one else had ever heard of? 'Young' is a word that still seems to follow me around and trip me up when I least suspect it.

When I talked to a friend of mine about this, she wondered aloud why the word 'young' always accompanied such directives. Good ideas came from older and more experienced people all the time, and in any case, wouldn't having a variety of voices at the table guarantee the best variety of ideas? She had a point. We always put modifiers in front of ourselves, and I'm no exception to that. 'Young' is a modifier I can't claim forever, but what I'm focusing on here are the expectations behind that word. It's the same with what school you went to or what you studied at university. The expectation that all creative writing students write beautiful sentences and all [Korean]

English graduates speak perfect English is inhibiting, if anything. It creates unnecessary pressure.

It's also why I usually don't reveal what I studied at university, if I can help it. My older sister is the same way. Having studied singing at the Seoul Institute of the Arts, she is taken for granted if she delivers a good performance but heavily criticised if she happens to hit a sour note. She lives in constant fear of being judged harshly. Many people must feel this way. It's why we can't enjoy the things we chose to study because we loved them. It's why some would rather find the nearest mouse hole to hide in than take the chance to develop their interests.

Today I deleted my school and work information on Facebook, because I wanted to erase the modifiers that followed my name. Displaying my school and occupation gave me brief feelings of superiority, but they also made me feel insecure. I hate the fact that I'm not a great writer despite my studies, that I haven't read everything despite working at a publishing house. These modifiers can never explain the whole of a person. The person I've been the most jealous of at work – she's a fantastic illustrator, a terrific writer, has a rich emotional life, is pretty and has a lovely personality – graduated from a provincial university. And I'm ashamed to admit that I tried to assuage my feelings of inferiority by comparing my academic CV to hers. *Oh, she didn't go to as prestigious a school as*

I thought, I found myself thinking, grasping at straws to feel as superior as possible.

Even as I'm aware of these thought processes in myself, I still feel the gaze of others through the modifiers that have been conferred upon me, and I still find myself unable to escape that gaze. When a person I was jealous of turned out to have gone to a lower-tier school, I felt relief, and a person I had not thought much of suddenly seemed much smarter once I heard where they went to school – then the self-criticism that followed my guilt over these stupid thoughts. I truly want to change how I am. And I believe I can change. Nowadays, I don't know where my closest friends at work went to school. Nor do I feel like I want to know. I haven't changed completely, but it's happening little by little. I want to focus on the parts that are changing, and to keep hoping. Hoping there will come a day when we can all feel good about ourselves regardless of modifiers.

DREAM

I had a lingering dream set in the past. My mother and older sister were there. There were others, but I don't remember them. I wanted to snap a photo of my mother as a young woman and lifted my camera, but she would not enter the frame. Because the past is past. Because we exist in a space only briefly, and then we disappear. We can't even pin things down in a photo, I thought.

But we were having fun. Even if we couldn't record it or remember it afterwards, we were happy just because we were together there. It was quite a fascinating scene: my sister and me as girls, my mother without a single wrinkle. Even as I write this, the dream is fading from my memory and I can no longer see her face. I wish I could see Mother's young, radiant face one more time. A sad and beautiful dream.

GRANDMOTHER

Grandmother never had much to say. She never said bad things about others, either. When I asked her where Father would fall as a son-in-law on a scale from 0 to 100, she asked me what I would give him; I very confidently gave him a zero. Grandmother kept smiling and evading my question, which made me ask, 'If I was to bring a man like Father and tell you I was marrying him, would you let me?' To which she finally answered, '. . . No.' She's hilarious.

While I was staying with her, I had to go downtown for something one day and we were walking the streets of Suncheon together. Grandmother suddenly asked, 'It must be boring for you here, you must want to leave all the time, right?' I assured her that that wasn't the case; I was staying briefly only because I wasn't sure I'd have the opportunity to travel on my own again. Still, perhaps out of guilt, I kept insisting I wasn't leaving because I was bored. To be honest, she wasn't completely wrong. It's just that when I talk to my grandmother, our conversation often ends in silence and there really isn't much to do where she lives. Nor do I want to be staring at my phone when I never get to see her. I want to talk with my grandmother, and she used to tell me all sorts of fun stories, but she seems to have run dry of stories these days – but it's also true that I may not have another chance to travel on my own for a long time.

In any case, we continued to walk together, and arrived at a community centre, which happened to be putting on some kind of festival. There were lots of seniors there. I gave Grandmother a hug, telling her, 'Be well, Grandma,' and dropped her off. When I turned back, I saw her waving at me, urging me to be on my way. I kept looking back until she was just a dot in the distance.

I remembered a conversation we had the other day. 'Grandma, what was the happiest moment for you?' And she answered that she was alone every day so how could she have a happy moment.

I then asked, shyly, 'Are you happy that I'm here then?'

'Absolutely, I'm very pleased.'

'But not happy?' I countered.

'Being pleased is being happy.'

My heart hurts whenever I think of her, and I hate that it does because it feels like pity, but I've decided to think of it as love. And such feelings are perhaps inevitable when it comes to love.

After our company's welcoming event, I happened to bump into the CEO. Normally I'm afraid of adults (despite my having become one), and powerful adults even more so. So you can imagine how extra scary the CEO is to me. He asked me what my ambition was for this year, and when I hesitated, he wondered aloud if the word 'ambition' was too fancy a word. Which is why I said my modest goal of the year was to have a healthy body and mind. Thinking that I needed to say something about work, I added that I would also like to edit a bestseller. But why did I find that so embarrassing to say? It was so clichéd and stupid. So obvious. I'm not even interested in bestsellers. I only wanted to get out of the conversation as quickly as possible and I couldn't do that if I'd just said my goal was to put out good books – he would only interrogate me on what I thought was a good book. But my answer was embarrassing. I really wish I could be a more candidly honest person. I envy those who can answer questions adroitly and without guise.

MY AUNT

Yesterday my mother went to the hospital for her regular check-up. It was also the day Grandmother was supposed to come up to Seoul. Mother was always afraid of unfamiliar surroundings, and the thought of her and Grandmother getting lost inside a big hospital annoyed me so much that I took a half-day from the office and accompanied them.

Grandmother comes up once every three months for a check-up and to fill her prescription meds. There's no big hospital where she lives. Grandmother used to go to a hospital in Ansan, then the Yeongdeungpo District in Seoul, and now she goes all the way up to Ilsan in the northern suburbs. My youngest aunt used to take my grandmother up to Ilsan once every three months, and then the responsibility passed on to my eldest aunt, then to my mother.

My Aunt Goara, who lives around Ilsan, will not pick up her phone. Mother doesn't know why, and Grandmother sadly said it was probably because she didn't want to deal with her. Mother looked conflicted at that. I fumed; it wasn't as if Grandmother was coming up once a week, it was only once every three months!

But then I began to recall more things about Aunt Goara. She was the one who read a lot, who always took care of Grandmother, and her nieces and nephews, and who had now distanced herself from the family.

Aunt Goara had been special to me and my sisters as well. Whenever we needed a car, she, rather than my father, would drive us around and tell us many things about the world in a way that we as children could understand. Whenever Father hit Mother, we never called our eldest aunt in tears but our Aunt Goara, even though they both lived the same distance away from us. Thinking back, Aunt Goara was our oasis. She understood us better than our own mother; she was a second mother to us.

These memories made me think how the words 'That person has changed' are completely useless in some cases; it finally occurred to me that to expect someone to always be a certain way or consistently do a certain thing can be a huge burden on them.

When life becomes something one just lives through, when the demands of survival take up all of our time and effort, leaving no strength for any other demands, and when time rushes by drying up or rotting whatever we have had to neglect, expecting someone to carry on being the same is truly too much of a burden.

Aunt Goara's life was something we didn't pay enough attention to, something that we let slip from our own lives. I am sure of this now. When we lose our sense of hope in our own lives, we can also lose the many touchstones in our lives. We don't want to do anything, be part of anything, or *want* to be with anyone. All of our desire for relationships disappears, and we become totally isolated.

Once I realised it, this truth seemed self-evident, and I thought I should've known better as someone who was more aware of Aunt Goara's life than most people. But I had shamefully been annoyed at her for not being there for her family one last time. I tried ignoring my shame, but it quickly spread into my body and the next day turned into physical nausea, like some punishment.

Rebecca Solnit said in *The Faraway Nearby* that empathy is an act of imagination. If I don't plant the seed in myself, it will never grow. Which is why some people never seem to understand the lives of others. But the only way to create something inside me that is not there to begin with is through imagination. You've got to learn how to empathise, to imagine.

I used to treat empathy as something very difficult, and shut myself off from the things that didn't affect me emotionally. But surely to create something in me that didn't exist before and to extend emotional solidarity to another person is one of the rites of adulthood. We are so far, and yet so near to so many people.

To learn about and imagine the emotions that I don't understand or immediately empathise with: that is the affection I extend to others, and the only way to ensure that what's inside of us doesn't dry up or rot.

Maybe complete empathy is impossible, but we can certainly keep trying. I believe that trying in the face of this knowledge is the most worthwhile thing we can do.

And so, I made a decision to seek out those I could come to a common understanding with. Those I have always held affection for, but for one reason or other, turned away from in the course of life.

MY DOGS, MY ALL

Boogie is three. Suji is nine. Juding is fifteen. When Juding was little, I called him Rocket Juding. The way he sprang out of the elevator once the doors opened was just like he'd blasted off, he was so quick.

Whenever we opened the front door after a long day, he would walk right into our legs, tapping our knees with his front paws until we picked him up. He always knew when we were eating something, bounding up to us the moment we'd take out a sweet potato or open a biscuit packet. Also when the fried chicken arrived, or the grilled meat.

When he was little, his tiny heart would beat in perfect time, his eyes sparkled, his nose was wet, and the bottoms of his feet and tummy were still pink, smelling like babies. No one taught him to, but he always went to the toilet in the bathroom or the veranda. Sometimes he would go up to the veranda doors and tap them, asking us to open them. Rarely, he barked. He got jealous a lot.

We've taken all of these behaviours for granted for years and years, but lately these quirks have been disappearing and are now almost gone. I don't need to put him on a leash anymore as Juding walks even slower than I do, and he's so deaf he can't hear me opening the front door and no longer comes bounding up to greet me. Only when I interrupt his sleep with an 'I'm home' does he suddenly spring awake with a start. He doesn't drink milk and sometimes refuses meat, and doesn't seem to care what he eats anymore. His heartbeat sounds irregular, his eyes are pale and his nose dry, and the pigment on his feet and tummy has blackened. He doesn't tap the veranda doors anymore to ask to pee. It's been forever since I last heard him bark. And he sleeps so much I'm almost afraid . . . His whitened beard puts fear in my heart. Probably because I am in denial that the poor dear is an old dog now.

Watching the young antics of Suji and Boogie makes me think of the old Juding, which breaks my heart. I realise more than ever that Juding's time on earth is so much faster and more fleeting than mine. These are my thoughts when I see the two young ones gather at my feet when I'm eating something, or see their ears perk up even when I whisper to them.

I feel too young to have seen the life and death of a living sentient being. All beginnings and endings feel so heavy to me. I am too much of a worrier to focus on the happiness of the moment. Even as I lie on the sofa surrounded by my three dogs, I feel that our time is precious and happy, and our futures that much more fearful and dark.

I think about the word 'weak'. I'm weak, which is why I fear and hate anything that is weak. But I still want to have these dogs in my life more than anything else. I would never send them away from me.

TOGETHERNESS

There are days when I wish I were numb, when I'm desperate to feel nothing. I want to be simple and cold and totally without feeling. Empathy has a large presence in my life, and it can cast a very long shadow. I can be watching a television drama or a movie, listening to a song or looking at a photograph, listening to someone's story or writing my own, and my heart and mood will sink. Like a punctum they pierce me without context, a feeling I am very used to now and tired of.

Which is why I put up walls and tried to keep myself safe for so long. I thought I had built a shelter for myself, but I had only locked myself up in a prison (as much as I hate using that metaphor). I thought I would be happier but that wasn't the case. I wanted constant reassurances that I hadn't been wrong, and I obsessed over even the smallest of affections. I kept wondering aloud why I was the way I was, and my cynicism towards others deepened. I had wanted to be a cool, rational person, but once I had cooled down, my world froze. Every place I put my finger on would ache. I was angry and frustrated.

It's obvious now that I think about it. Fencing myself inside myself, not meeting anyone, not sharing anyone, that's just making a castle out of ice. My focus was on the coldness of others, and that left my life with no warmth at all.

All kinds of negative emotions kept rising in me, leaving me unable to breathe. I needed to find a way to let them out.

That's when I first sought therapy. I could immediately sense that sharing, which was something I had no trouble doing when I was younger, had already become much more difficult – but once we began to talk, I could feel everything flowing out of me. I had thought I only needed one person to share things with, but I was wrong.

From that moment on, I often shared my thoughts and feelings with family, friends, colleagues and even strangers, listening to their stories in turn and filling myself with new air. Not in a fake-friendly way but in a sincere way, with all my heart. It felt like I was balancing out some of the self-consciousness and self-pity in my feelings.

In the end, a better way to live is to live among others, something I felt when I went on a holiday with my family, the first in a long while. Togetherness means altruism, and altruism is what saves us from selfishness. Because it begins with me and ends with everyone. Others are bound to be moved by the fact that you want to be with them, that you want to understand them, that you can't do without them. Being together, misunderstanding each other, sharing with each other, growing further apart from each other, all these things help us live out our present moment. I wonder if this is our way of comforting ourselves through the darkness that is our world.

I am always at war. Me against dozens, or hundreds. It's impossible to count more than that, after a certain point. The more your enemies grow, the more exhausted you become, and you lose morale. Or perhaps you never had much morale in the first place. You cannot win, and you cannot even think of winning. Life is as messy as a bag whose owner never cleans it out. You have no idea when you might reach in and pull out a piece of old trash, and you're afraid someone is going to look through your bag someday. Maybe your 'baggage' is like an old bag, too. You toss it around any which way, not caring how worn it gets or where it lands, and no one notices. You can't afford a new bag so you carefully and painstakingly hold it so the rough patches don't show. I've been scoffing at my own bag metaphor just now, but I don't think it's too far off either.

When I happen to be writing on the bus and someone stands in front of me, I stop writing. Their eyes seem to be looking down right at my phone screen. I'm afraid they'll be reading my thoughts, these thoughts that can be as dark as the most private parts of my diary. I consider my public persona as the cover for what is underneath, a membrane no light can seep through. The inner thoughts that do not make it through the membrane fester inside of me. Which is why my thoughts are never clean, and it's hard to find a good thought in my inner rot. Just like muddy water filtered through a mesh still comes out brown, the thoughts I've refined and refined again are thick with darkness. I try to hide this through decorative words and metaphors. All this refining and decorating may look good, but it's empty packaging.

I love the innocence of bright and honest people and adore the writings of positive thinkers, but I fear that I will never be able to find myself among them. I have trouble both accepting my own darkness and throwing myself into the light. I yearn to be valued by others, to be loved unconditionally by others, but I feign disinterest in others despite my substantial interest in them. My faking creates more faking, and that goes on to create even more faking, to the point where I can't tell whether I am faking or not faking, whether these are my real feelings and thoughts or the packaged ones. My mind wants to be completely calm while my heart is anything but, a state of affairs that throws me off balance, into turmoil, which shows on my face. My twisted face creates twisted behaviours. I try to shove 'properness' into my twisted mind and body to correct it but end up with a Jenga stack of a self that soon comes crashing down.

Despite knowing I can never attain perfect freedom, I keep plodding through on this road. The end of the road is erased. I try to create a path where there is no path, but no matter how much I pace that rough ground, it refuses to become a path. My toes keep kicking against the rocks.

FICTION

The only real talent I have is putting others down. Like a lamp in the dark night, I can see other people's weaknesses all too clearly, and I used to enjoy pointing them out and attacking them. If someone were to ask me why that was, I couldn't really answer; I guess I just didn't know myself very well. And because I didn't know myself very well, I couldn't stand others who seemed to be fully confident in who they were, it made me breathless and nauseous. Watching them be disconcerted or break down would console me. What a pitiful life I used to have.

I place more importance on attitude than on character. Actually, I believe that attitude contains character. That honesty, which is an attitude, shows in the smallest of things and the most insignificant of moments. I tend to look closely at the eyes, gestures, speech and movements of a person in trying to discern them.

When I love someone, I have many questions for them, but these questions are not always asked in words. Sometimes, they're expressed in gestures. The chin resting on a hand as they look towards me, the eyes concentrating on my mouth, the nodding, the hue and shading of their responses as they punctuate my story. I pour out my heart to them and answer questions they ask me. Every word becomes a question, and every word becomes an answer. This is what it feels like to have someone to whom you could reveal everything to, even when you're not asked.

On the other hand, there are those many questions that we simply swallow and never ask. I think people are shy, perhaps not everyone and not all the time, but there are definitely many moments where our throats close up or we worry about what other people will think of us, and so we don't ask. My friends call me the Queen of Curiosity with all my questions, but even those questions are the result of having picked through a much larger pile. Even when so many of the questions that do get asked in the world are so invasive and heavy and private and silly and obvious.

This is why I like people who draw answers from me without even asking a question, or who seem to answer my questions before I even ask them. This connection gives me the warmest of feelings.

But I do feel a bit bereft. Where do the questions we've swallowed end up? Do they scatter somewhere or sink deep inside of us? Do they manifest in strange behaviours or habits? And wouldn't such silence come in the way of making deeply felt connections with others? That's what I fear the most.

ROMANTICISM AND CYNICISM

We often judge the whole by a single moment. A person may be very bookish and intellectual, but if they happen to be scrolling through their Instagram feed in front of me, I might judge them to be superficial. Which is why I feel that liking someone at first sight or the concept of destiny is a romanticised self-rationalisation. It's all just timing. A moment where I happen to look special and you happen to look special – just a coincidence. But these beautiful coincidences are also responsible for most of our life's relationships. Which is also why there's no need to be cynical about them.

In any case, I tend to go back and forth between romanticism and cynicism. Crossing those barriers between hot and cold, I forget the lukewarm boredom of life; that lukewarm state is what I fear the most. Unable to return to feeling hot or cold, to be numb within a state of room temperature. In that state, we're nothing better than dead.

A NOTE ON THE AUTHOR

Born in 1990, Baek Sehee studied creative writing in university before working for five years at a publishing house. For ten years, she received psychiatric treatment for dysthymia (persistent mild depression), which became the subject of her essays, and then *I Want to Die but I Want to Eat Tteokbokki*, books one and two. Her favorite food is tteokbokki, and she lives with her rescue dog Jaram.

A NOTE ON THE TRANSLATOR

Anton Hur was longlisted for the 2022 International Booker Prize for his translations of Bora Chung's *Cursed Bunny* and Sang Young Park's *Love in the Big City*. He also enjoys tteokbokki.

A NOTE ON THE TYPE

The text of this book is set in Linotype Sabon, a typeface named after the type founder, Jacques Sabon. It was designed by Jan Tschichold and jointly developed by Linotype, Monotype and Stempel in response to a need for a typeface to be available in identical form for mechanical hot metal composition and hand composition using foundry type.

Tschichold based his design for Sabon roman on a font engraved by Garamond, and Sabon italic on a font by Granjon. It was first used in 1966 and has proved an enduring modern classic.